Sowerby's Road

Sowerby's Road

Adventures of a driven mind

Best to John &
The Girls. —

26/11/03

Garry Sowerby

Odyssey International Ltd.

National Library of Canada Cataloguing in Publication Data
Sowerby, Garry, 1950-
    Sowerby's Road : *Adventures of a driven mind*

ISBN 0-9733358-0-7

1. Sowerby, Garry – Journeys
2. Automobile travel – Anecdotes   I. Title

GV1023.S68 2003   796.7'092   C2003-904922-1

Cover and book design: Michael Doyle, *Allegro Visual Communications*
Cover photography: Garry Sowerby and Graham McGaw

Published by:
Odyssey International Limited
P.O. Box 22-177 Bayers RPO
Halifax, Nova Scotia
Canada   B3L 4T7

tel: 1 902 455-8258
fax: 1 902 455-9557
odyssey@hfx.eastlink.ca
www.adventuredrive.ca
www.sowerbysroad.com

10 9 8 7 6 5 4 3 2 1
Printed and bound in Canada.

*For my father, Lee,
who taught me to look beyond the potholes.*

Acknowledgments

The events described in this book would never have taken place without the efforts of countless people, corporations and organizations in more than 75 countries around the world. For their consideration and decency in providing assistance and safe passage, I would like to express my deepest gratitude and sincere thanks.

I would however, like to offer special thanks to the following people.

My mother and father, Edith and Lee, whose wit, curiosity and love of life provided me with the fortitude to trust my instincts while realizing my capabilities and limitations. My three daughters Lucy, Natalie and Layla who have given me purpose, love and joy.

Ken Langley for his friendship and spirit, key ingredients in our decision to go for the Road in the first place.

John Rock, Frank Cronin, Art Christy, Stew Low, Doug MacDonald, Rick Lee, Nick Reilly, Gus Buenz, Phil Kling and other folk at various divisions of General Motors Corporation who saw reason to come on the ride; Jim Fitzhenry and Ken Barratt at Volvo Canada Limited who trusted us in the beginning.

Talented and dedicated road cronies Beverly Barrett, Derrick Bemister, Kevin Boales, Colin Bryant, Tim Cahill, Heather Capstick, Jon Clark, Jane Davis, Kathy DeLorenzo, John DeMont, Peter Duffy, Jeff Fish, Jennifer Giese, Sandy Huntley, Rob Hutchison, Richard Jacobs, Tom Khattar, Ron King, Luc Lapointe, Finlay MacDonald, Helen MacMillan, Graham McGaw, Lara McLean, Gerry McNeil, Al McPhail, Rik Paul, Bill Rumsey, Peter Schlay, Janet Shorten, Paul Solomons, Larry Sowerby, Joe Tippett, Ken Trites and Catherine Tuck.

Alan McPhee at Formula Publications who encouraged me to write the columns that form the basis of *Sowerby's Road*. And to Bill McLauchlan, whose suggestion to do this book gave me the confidence to go ahead.

Mike Doyle at Allegro Visual Communications whose skill, patience and imagination made the production of this book a trip in itself. His wife, Gail, for her humour and tenacious editing sessions.

And to Lisa Calvi, my business partner, wife and soulmate for kindness, love and unwavering commitment.

Garry Sowerby

Contents

You Have Strange Job, Yes?   Chapter 1

The Blur of Woods and Rock   Chapter 5

Three Parts Horn, One Part Driving   Chapter 6

Anyone Can Do That   Chapter 7

Preface

In the Fall of 1977, I picked up my old college buddy Ken Langley at his apartment in Ottawa. He had a week off from his job as an Executive Assistant for a Member of Parliament and I had taken leave from my job as a Test and Evaluation Officer for the Canadian Armed Forces.

We were both excited about the impending overnight road trip to Nova Scotia where we would visit family, party with old friends and perhaps even run into an old flame. Ken and I were both single, had challenging jobs and liked to travel. But as the sun set over the Ottawa River, the last thing I expected from the all-nighter was the twist of fate that would throw my life into a 25-year journey of proportions I could never have imagined.

Rolling into the port city of Halifax the next afternoon Ken and I were deep into the concept of the ultimate road trip... *to drive around the world faster than anyone had ever driven before.*

We would have to quit our well-paying jobs, set up a company, Odyssey International Limited, to raise corporate sponsorship and maintain faith in our abilities to take on a task that would eventually propel us onto the front cover of the *Guinness Book of World Records*.

The success of that 74-day trip through 18 countries and 5 continents delighted our sponsors and calmed the nerves of our friends and relatives. Everyone we knew shared our jubilation except for the bankers holding loans for the $110,000 shortfall on our $400,000-drive into the record books.

We were left with three choices. Go bankrupt, get jobs and pay off the debt over the next twenty years or develop another event that might furnish us with the financial ability to pacify the jittery bankers.

We opted for adventure and in 1984 went on to set a new speed record for the fastest drive from the Cape Agulhas, South Africa to the northern tip of Europe at North Cape, Norway. We returned home to a hero's welcome with nine bullet holes in our GMC Suburban truck from an ambush in Kenya, tales of a daring transit through the Iran-Iraq war and advertising contracts with enough clout to wipe out our lingering debt.

In 1985, Ken left Odyssey to pursue a law career and I found myself at a cross roads. Get a 'real job' or take on the last of the three internationally recognized long distance driving records, the *Pan American Challenge*. The lure of the *Challenge* outweighed risk and responsibility, and in 1987, Montana writer Tim Cahill and I managed to halve the existing record for the drive from the bottom to the top of the Americas.

At the end of that quest I was firmly entrenched into the world of driving adventures and have since been on the forefront of conceptualizing and implementing another 60 driving events of varying scope and purpose. I have, with the help of countless people and organizations, managed to have my cake and eat it too by conducting myself with a few basic rules. Do what you say you will do. Nothing is free. Not much is easy.

This book is not a chronological history of my life on the road. It does not attempt to tell the complete story either. The following 50 stories are slices of what I have taken from The Road and what it has given back through 25 years of motorized wanderings around the planet.

I do not own any highways or country trails. *Sowerby's Road* is a trip through time, a trip that has provided an opportunity to experience much more than I ever anticipated.

To learn. To trust. To be trusted.

And to drive.

Preface

Dawn, approaching the Muchinga Mountains, Zambia, Africa

"*So come, on with our voyage now, we're wasting time.*"

Homer, *The Odyssey*

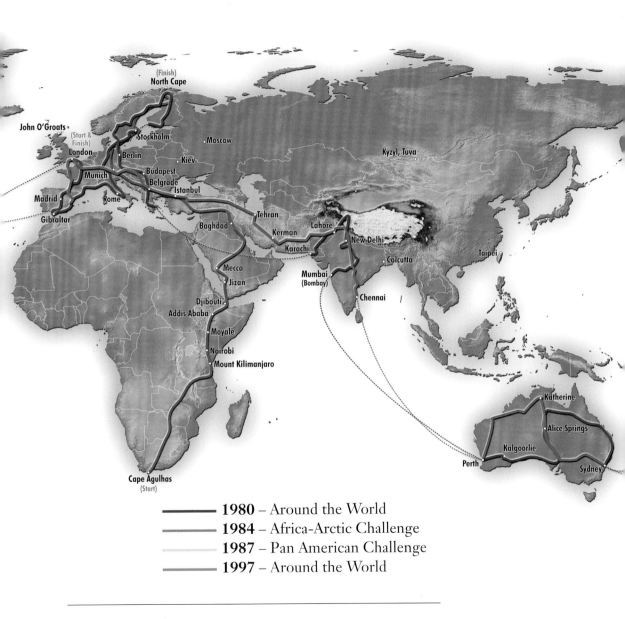

1980 – Around the World
1984 – Africa-Arctic Challenge
1987 – Pan American Challenge
1997 – Around the World

Street scene, Calcutta, India

Chapter 1 *You Have Strange Job, Yes?*

*B*id farewell and make sure everyone, including the guy with the 50-calibre machine gun, understands that you understand that everyone understands that you are movin' on.

1. Lucy Panzer and the Fortune Teller

Not much sleep that Fall night. About two or three hours I reckon. But it was worth it since I was having such a great time with an old friend I hadn't seen in years.

Of course it was a Road Trip. The sixteen hours from Nashua, New Hampshire to Halifax, Nova Scotia gave us a chance to get caught up on some of the outrageous times we spent together back in the 80s when, for a while, we were inseparable.

Sure she had aged a bit, but she was as spirited as when I was last with her at a Hollywood Gala years earlier. She still turned heads wherever we went and although she smoked for the first few hours, by the time we hit Maine, she put the habit to rest.

Perhaps she realized how tense it was making me, or maybe she was getting used to the new injector pump they bolted into the cleavage of her V-8 Detroit Diesel before she left Los Angeles for our New Hampshire rendezvous. Yes, Lucy Panzer, the eight thousand-pound 1984 GMC Suburban Ken Langley and I finessed our way through a lifetime of dicey situations between South Africa and North Cape, Norway still had the

I felt like I had slipped into a time warp. All those toggle switches.

goods. Even after four years of hanging around Beverly Hills' prestigious Petersen Automotive Museum, she was still unrefined and noisy with craggy road manners. But for her size, she handled surprisingly well.

I had slipped into a time warp. All those toggle switches. The forest of antennae on the roof. The smell in there, like crawling into a favourite old travel trunk. Yellowed press kits featuring fresh-faced Ken and I posed in front of Mount Kilimanjaro with 'NO FEAR' written all over our faces. That favourite John Prine tape hanging out of the tape deck, Springsteen's *Born to Run* in the glove box with the sticky latch. Under the seat, the rock we used to prop up the tire jack on that rutted road in Kenya's Kasuit Desert after bandits shot out our rear tires.

I had run into the venerable beast by surprise. The folks at General Motors had invited me to one of their media events in New Hampshire so I flew down and spent a day driving trucks around road courses set up at the New Hampshire International Speedway.

I had a ball. When else do you get a chance to drive a fuel oil delivery truck, a tandem dump truck, a moving van and another dozen variants around all morning? In the afternoon it was light truck time where I found myself blasting around the track in a 6-litre 300-horsepower Sierra pick-up truck. It had 25% fewer parts than its predecessor. It was fast,

quiet and smooth. It was a far cry from Lucy Panzer.

At the end of the day, the organizers said they had shipped in a surprise for me. It was hidden around back of one of the pit garages.

"All right," I thought. "A new Sierra. Or perhaps a Yukon to haul my family around in"

My wife, Lisa Calvi, and our three daughters would be really impressed when Dad pulled into the yard in a spanking-new GMC truck. They would cheer and realize I really *did* have good friends in far-off places.

Then I saw her. Lucy Panzer, listing slightly to port and riddled with bullet holes from that day in Kenya. With her scrapes and scratches showing through the fresh wax job, the truck reminded me of a scrappy puppy waiting for its owner at the dog groomers. And as I slid behind the wheel and fired her up, my want of shiny new metal evaporated.

That night, at a dinner in Searles Castle, a fortune teller read my palm. She told me all the good stuff. I'd live a long life. The relationship with my wife would last forever. My children loved me. They would live a long life too.

The next day as I drove through the Maine woods on my way to Halifax, a flood of memories filled my head. The wind whistle from the CB antennae. The growl from the special air intake installed for desert operations. The air horns. They were all still there.

I thought about how life had unfolded since that harrowing day in the Kasuit Desert back in 1984. I thought about all the roads, the meetings, the inconceivable places. The people along the way. My family.

Then I remembered the fortune teller's parting words.

"One more thing. You have strange job, yes?"

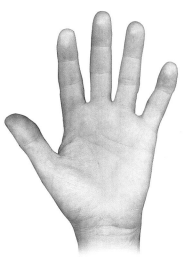

Below left: *Sunrise over Mount Kilimanjaro, Tanzania, Africa*

Below right: *Heading north through Kenya's Kasuit Desert, after being ambushed by Shifta bandits.*

2. Motley Crew at Faaker See

I had driven non-stop down the autobahns from the German port of Hamburg on the North Sea into Austria. It was a pristine September morning in 1982 and I was in need of a good sleep when I pulled up to the tourist information centre an hour south of Salzburg.

Nestled around a series of lakes at the base of the Austrian Alps, the stunningly beautiful area had nothing on Katrina, the slim and statuesque blond who greeted me. In a sexy, *Spy Who Loved Me* voice, she reviewed a registration package for the five-day convention I was about to attend.

Katrina told me I was one of 60 Guinness World Record holders registered along with as many reporters from around the world. The

Englishman John Moss holds back a 490 cc Yamaha motorcycle with his teeth.

Austrian Tourist Association would provide accommodations at resorts surrounding Faaker See, a crystalline alpine lake a short drive away. A slew of media events was scheduled throughout the convention where record holders could strut their stuff.

I was wondering how to demonstrate driving around the world at an Austrian press conference when Katrina folded up her notes and stood directly in front of me. She was gorgeous.

"We go Faak now?" she asked. Her dreamy blue eyes seemed to detect my confusion.

"We go where?" I struggled to make sense of what she wanted.

"To Faak, so you can check into the hotel. It is a beautiful lake," she added, as I collected my composure.

The next morning, Norris McWhirter who, with twin Ross, founded the Guinness Book of Records in 1955, welcomed the unlikely collection of humanity. As he spoke, I thumbed through Katrina's material trying to figure out who was who. Across the table Roger Bourbon, who ran marathons in a waiter's uniform carrying bottled water on a serving tray, was chatting with Sabra Starr, a belly dancer who could gyrate for 100 hours non-stop. Meanwhile Raino, a German, pulled a 6-inch high bicycle out of his briefcase and started circling the room as he would do all week whenever he had an audience.

Even at 6´ 2˝ tall, I'm dwarfed by the tallest man in the British Commonwealth, Chris Greener.

Later we stepped outside where Englishman John Moss clamped his teeth onto the end of a tow-rope. The other end was tied to the back of a snorting 490 cc Yamaha motorcycle. With John anchored to the front of a transport truck, the motorcycle hopelessly spun its rear wheel trying to escape the mighty molars of Mr. Moss. He later told me his teeth once held down a helicopter.

Over the next few days, I witnessed an unbalanced Englishman do 760 one-handed push-ups and met a flat-stomached chap who recorded 26,000 sit-ups. A gentleman known as the Flyer of Flemsbury made swan diving across four kitchen tables look like child's play. I hung out with the hungriest flame-eating lady, who I suspected wore an asbestos wig, a woman who could eat 100 yards of spaghetti in less than 30 seconds and lanky 7 1/2-foot giant Chris Greener. The smartest man in the world was there and wanted to know if the Volvo we raced around the world had been 'souped up'.

Top: *Donna Maiello ate more spaghetti in 30 seconds than anyone in the world.*

Middle: *World's largest pillow.*

Bottom: *How low can you go? Not as low as Denise Culp who held the world record for 'roller-limbo'.*

Frenchman Michel Lotto earned his nickname, Mr. Mangetout, after eating an entire Cessna airplane.

"Geeez, what was the worst part?" I asked, trying to wrap my head around his obsession.

"Aaaahhh, the tires!" He went on to tell me about his plans to eat an Austin Mini. More tires!

On the last night of the conference, Lufthansa threw a big party. Everyone feasted on old-world delights washed down with plenty of draft beer. There were lots of laughs. During one of my many washroom visits, I was chatting at the urinal with Jim Selby, a *National Enquirer* photographer, when Chris the Giant came in. Jim slipped me one of those 'Enquiring-minds-want-to-know' looks as Chris approached the urinal beside us. But to our dismay, instead of relieving himself, the giant broke wind, about-faced and stomped out.

The photographer seemed depressed. Quite a missed opportunity from his point of view I imagined.

"Don't feel bad, Jim," I offered, looking for a silver lining, "at least we heard a Giant fart."

About midnight, we were taken back to our hotel. The manager invited me, the Giant, the Brain and Raino into the bar for a night cap. Raino pulled out his bike while I learned an important life lesson: don't sit in an Austrian bar trying to out-drink a Giant and then go call your girlfriend in Toronto. And don't fall asleep arguing with her about insignificant trivia with the phone line open.

Morning came quickly. I was dry with a pounding headache. There was a telephone bill for $375 under the door. At breakfast on the patio, the Guinness people explained their book was in itself a record for the largest-selling copyrighted book in the world. As they pointed out that the previous year's sales were equivalent to 118 stacks of books, each as high as Mount Everest, I scanned the gathering. The fire eating lady was trying to break her record of eating 6,670 flames in 2 hours. The smell of the torch was getting gross. Donna Maiello was trying to down another 100 yards of spaghetti in under 30 seconds. Sauce was flying everywhere.

Willem Klein, the human computer was sitting at my table. He could extract the 13th root from a 100 digit number in his head. I asked if he could translate my around-the-world record into minutes. He told me it was 107,011 and asked if I wanted to know the square root.

I escaped breakfast and headed to the summer toboggan run for the last event of the conference where teams were trying for the best time down the metal run. They were all there… the belly dancer, Mr. Push-up and even Christian Patzig, the backward-sitting cyclist who peddled 113 kilometres using mirrors to steer while playing classical violin.

I was voted lead toboggan.

"Go faster." They all coaxed.

I did and then managed to loose control and flip the toboggan half way down the slope. It knocked the wind out of me. My baby finger is still crooked from the incident. I staggered to the bottom of the hill and asked Mr. Mangetout if he was giving it a try. He declined, citing the havoc the toboggan run would wreak on the 21 bullets he had for breakfast.

Back at the hotel I dutifully approached the front desk to pay for the blabbering, snoring telephone call. The manager, looking a little schnapps green himself, refused the money.

"It is on zee house," he offered. "If I had not passed around zee free schnapps, I am sure zee phone call would have been shorter."

Out of the corner of my eye, I could see Raino opening his briefcase in front of a busload of Japanese tourists.

Great place, this Faaker See.

"*Round the World Driving*
The fastest circumnavigation embracing more than an equator's length of driving (24, 901.47 road miles 40,075.0 km) is one in 74 days 1 hr 11 min by Garry Sowerby (driver) and Ken Langley (navigator) of Canada from 6 Sept to 19 Nov 1980 in a Volvo 245 westwards from Toronto, Canada through 4 continents and 23 countries. The distance covered was 42,754.8 km 26,561.0 miles."

Guinness Book of Records 1983 Edition, Guinness Superlatives Ltd., 1982

3. Border Patrol

Six days after the horrific World Trade Center and Pentagon attacks of September 11, 2001, Lisa and I were scheduled to fly from Halifax to Miami for a week. We weren't sure about taking a trip in the days following the destruction, but finally agreed to proceed with the plan, which had been in place for months.

I had a hard time getting to sleep the night before leaving. The unlikely event of ending up on a hijacked airliner wasn't the cause of my insomnia. It was imagining the reception at the U.S. border when I presented a stamp-filled passport that included current visas to enter Pakistan and Iran. An entry from a recent family vacation in Cuba didn't seem like an asset either.

With absolutely nothing to hide, we approached the immigration officer.

"Where do you live? Where are you going? Who do you work for? How long will you be in Miami?" His questions were fast and furious as he thumbed through our passports. Then, as if a switch had been flipped, he smiled, wished us a pleasant trip and waved us through.

Border controls have always been something I like to view in the

rearview mirror, especially during one of those timed endurance drives that have taken me through some of the world's most desolate border posts. The knot starts about three hours from the frontier. Things get quiet in the car except for isolated bouts of small talk punctuated by nervous laughter as we reassure each other that our papers are indeed in order.

Thoughtful interior goodie placement is advisable. Fish out a pack of Marlboros and lay them on the dashboard in plain view. Make sure the registered owner of the vehicle is driving. Tidy up the interior and hang an attractive souvenir pen out of your shirt pocket. Keep the *carton* of Marlboros and the case of souvenir pens out of sight.

Approaching the post, remove sunglasses so they can see you have eyeballs. Be friendly, but not overly. Attempt a word or two in the local language. Once cleared, move away slowly, nod a lot and smile. Bid farewell and make sure everyone, including the guy with the 50-calibre machine gun, understands that you understand that everyone understands that you are movin' on. Adjust the rearview mirror so you can see the post disappear. Grin.

I have never been good at knowing when a bribe might be in order, beyond the ones I offer my kids when good behaviour is essential. Once after a lengthy delay at the Romanian border, I clued in after an officer told me of the expensive testicle operation one of his children needed.

The bullet holes in our truck sometimes helped get us through borders.

Another time, my former partner, Ken Langley, and I took action after being stonewalled for hours by the Turks at the Iraq-Turkey frontier. They expressed zero interest in our story about attempting to set a world speed record for the fastest time from the southern tip of Africa to the northern tip of Europe. The nine bullet holes in our GMC Suburban from an ambush in Kenya didn't impress them either. Nor did the fact that we had just driven through a section of the Iran-Iraq war.

Finally one of them mentioned that a donation might hurry things up.

"How much?" I was assured fifty dollars would be sufficient.

"Do you take travellers cheques?" I asked.

He eyed the Thomas Cook Travellers Cheques logo on the front fender of our sponsor-decaled Suburban. There was a bullet hole through the word 'Cheques'.

Our new acquaintance smiled and informed us he had to go four kilometres down the road with us to a place where the transaction could be finalized. This seemed strange but, since it was in the direction of Istanbul, we agreed. A few minutes later, he told me to pull over and cut the lights on the side of the deserted highway.

We stumbled down an embankment beside the road. At the bottom, I could barely see the outline of a shack where we were led and introduced to ten or twelve Turks. They were sitting on a dirt floor in dim candlelight cleaning rifles, drinking mint tea and cracking jokes we couldn't understand.

We declined an offer of tea and hard biscuits in favour of getting down to business. I offered the travellers cheques while Ken engaged two gentlemen who could speak reasonable English.

The apparent boss, a large man dangling a cigarette between a gap in his teeth, told me the 'donation' was now elevated to one hundred dollars.

This seemed unfair. After all, a deal is a deal, but given our surroundings, I felt obliged to agree and produced five $20 cheques. I countersigned the first one, which Mr. Big carefully examined under a flickering candle. I knew it was too dark to see clearly so I held my breath and signed the last four with an entirely incorrect signature.

I passed on more offers for tea. Ken cut short his fellowship and we wasted no time getting up the embankment, into the Suburban and off into the darkness. I told Ken about my ploy to mess up the accounting system back at the bribe shack.

"Shouldn't have done that, Sowerby." He looked nervous in the faint glow of the dashboard lights. "Those guys were telling me about all their relatives that live along this road."

Just as I was getting a good case of the ebbi-jibbis, we saw the silhouettes of three people holding machine guns, waving us down from the side of the road. If they were bandits or the aforementioned relatives and we stopped, there would be trouble. If they were military or police and we didn't stop, that was trouble too.

Ken pulled up right beside them. They were young soldiers looking for a drive.

"Nah, not tonight." I choked out, as Ken drove away.

It was quiet in the truck the rest of the night, except for some small talk and the odd bout of nervous laughter.

A souvenir we bought at the Turkish border for a mere $100 in travellers cheques.

4. Miles of Milkshakes

I had been on airplanes between Tierra del Fuego, at the bottom of South America, and Canada for almost 24 hours. The ordeal involved a milk-run flight with 5 stops up to Buenos Aires and a red-eye to Miami. I then flew to Toronto and connected to a flight bound for Halifax.

Looking somewhat rumpled, I was just drifting off when a well-dressed man in the next seat offered to buy me a drink.

"Up in Toronto for a few days?" His name was Bill MacLennan and he was obviously in chat mode.

I explained I'd been in South America on a final planning trip before attempting to break the existing 56-day record for the fastest drive from the bottom to the top of the Americas. My goal was to complete the

23,500-kilometre route from the southern tip of Tierra del Fuego, Argentina to Prudhoe Bay, on Alaska's northern coast, in 25 days or less.

My partner, Montana-based writer Tim Cahill, and I would be driving a new 1988 GMC Sierra pick-up truck. The truck had been completely re-engineered for that year and General Motors was anxious to give it a real-world workout.

I learned Bill MacLennan was President of Farmers Co-Operative Dairy in Halifax. The dairy was about to begin marketing milkshakes in long-life Tetrapaks.

"If I give you $5,000, will you take a thousand milkshakes with you on your adventure?" He looked sincere.

"How about 500, and ship another 500 to Panama City for us to pick up on our way through?" I countered. A deal was struck.

Final preparations seemed endless. A mountain of paperwork had to be processed to obtain visas, letters of introduction, and customs documents for the truck. The Sierra was prepped with auxiliary lights, an air horn, winch and a snazzy paint job. A fibreglass cap over the pick-up bed covered a sleeping bunk, food, tools and emergency equipment. It also housed a 400-litre auxiliary fuel tank capable of filling the stock tank three times with the flick of a switch in the cab.

The truck could go 4,000 kilometres without stopping - plenty of range to dodge questionable fuel stops on the back roads of South America. We would be safe when we were moving.

However, one basic necessity was lacking. We couldn't figure how to get hot water into the cab of the truck at road speed, which was essential to 'cook' the freeze-dried food, we had on board. It was also needed for a fundamental road trip ingredient: coffee.

The day before embarking, Tim bought a water-heating coil that plugged into the cigarette lighter. He obviously had stumbled upon a piece of gear that would enable us to dine like royalty while blasting through the jungles of South America.

By the end of Day 1, we realized the heating coil did not live up to expectations. It took 20 minutes to heat a cup of water, which was deemed ineffective, considering the jarring driving conditions we were encountering.

Freeze-dried curried chicken whipped up with cold water was revolting and drinking cold instant coffee made with soda water produced a scary

We felt we would be safe when we were moving.

state of stomach turbulence. It soon became clear that the 500 milkshakes would be our best source of nourishment. At times, we mixed the frothy contents with instant coffee for a rudimentary version of café mocha.

Later, at one of the dozens of roadside controls, we stumbled on another use for the milkshakes. While Tim and I used primitive Spanish to explain what we were up to, heavily-armed police focused on the frosty Farmers milkshake I was drinking. Tim offered shakes to them as well as to a group of wide-eyed children who had gathered. The children cheered. The officers slapped us on the back.

Milkshake bribery sessions became ritual. We calculated that even if we drank 10 each a day, we still had 300 milkshakes to get us through the checkpoints between Argentina and Colombia.

In Peru, the pump that transferred fuel from the auxiliary tank went on the blink so I crawled over the tools, supplies and equipment stored under the fibreglass cap to rectify the problem. In the process, I crushed a few cases of shakes causing the milky froth to ooze into the cargo bed. The incident proved fortunate.

At the Colombian border, an official was unimpressed with our letters

Our first goal was to get through the muddy roads across the island of Tierra del Fuego, Argentina.

of introduction. He didn't care that the Tourism Minister in Honduras saw our record attempt as a good thing for people considering a visit to Tegucigalpa, its capital city. A cute picture of my 3-year-old daughter, Lucy, strategically placed beside the insurance papers didn't phase him either. He insisted we empty the contents of the Sierra to prove we were not carrying contraband or prohibited goods into his country.

When I opened the tailgate, Tim and I, along with a half dozen curious officers, reeled back in disgust. The putrid smell of the souring milkshakes from the crushed cases was repulsive.

"Pedazo de carne mala!" I accused Tim of being a bad piece of meat.

He returned the compliment and everyone broke up. We handed out strawberry shakes in the midst of the bizarre tailgate party and were soon on our way. Milkshakes had pulled us through again.

We reached the port city of Cartagena on Colombia's Caribbean coast in time to rendezvous with a container ship that took us through the Panama Canal. Delighted with our progress, we considered the worst was behind us.

As long as another 500 Farmers Milkshakes were waiting for us in Panama City.

5. Communication Breakdown

After a month on the road filing daily reports to sixth graders in Canada, Belgium and Japan, I was looking forward to the drive from Istanbul, Turkey to Frankfurt, Germany. The 3,000-kilometre route through Greece, Italy and Austria would avoid political problems in Eastern Europe and give me a chance to relax and reflect on what had just transpired.

Feedback from the children's teachers indicated the real-time geography experience had spurred a surprising level of classroom excitement. I had worked a few research exercises into the reports: math problems related to horn-blowing frequencies in downtown Istanbul, jet lag explanations and time zone quizzes. Drawing parallels between driving expeditions and recess marble tournaments had become the basis of the way I looked at things.

At the time, in 1995, interactively experiencing an event taking place thousands of kilometres away over the Internet was a relatively new concept. Doing it simultaneously in 12 different classrooms as part of a geography lesson made it even more novel to the few hundred participating students.

The lesson had been divided into three phases: getting from Canada to Istanbul, preparing for the expedition, and two weeks of exploring Turkey while interviewing sixth-grade Turkish students.

Before leaving Frankfurt, I asked my 'virtual' students for drive route suggestions. They would need to take into account the war in Serbia and fuel shortages in Romania. Only a few predicted my route over the Alps and down to Brindisi in southern Italy to catch the overnight ferry across the Adriatic Sea to Igoumenitsa, Greece. From there, I drove the Chevy Blazer that General Motors had provided a day and a half to Turkey where I spent a week holed up in sweltering Istanbul waiting for the techno-bits and the staff from GlobaLearn, a Connecticut-based educational company, to arrive.

In the meantime, Toronto videographer Jerry Vienneau flew in and we gathered equipment for the upcoming Turkish learning expedition. We went to meetings in ornate buildings. Jerry filmed street life. We even picked up a few Turkish words in the process. The rug shop 'sales consultants' we met by the daunting Blue Mosque suggested ways for us to remember basic vocabulary that would help us during our stay in Turkey.

They explained that the Turkish word for 'no' is *hayir* (pronounced higher) and 'yes' is *yavet* (pronounced like the woman's name Yvette). It was more difficult to master the word for 'good-bye', *Allahismarladik*. Realizing we would have trouble with that word, the rug shop language

tutors assured us that if we said 'Allah's-marble-dick' as fast as we could that it would pass for 'good bye'. It was hard to say without smiling a bit which made us look very friendly whenever we said good-bye.

After the folks from GlobaLearn arrived, we packed the Blazer with a mountain of computer and communications equipment, leaving barely enough room for Jerry and me. Then, with the GlobaLearn staff following in a rented van, we commenced our two-week driving tour of Turkey. Our goal was to document a day in the life of three Turkish children, each from a different socio-economic background.

The expedition, based on a 2,000-kilometre tour of west and central Turkey, took us to the thermal springs of Pamukkale and to the Cappadocia region where weird rock formations have produced a surrealistic land-of-the-Smurfs panorama. In each of the areas, we spent a day interviewing a child with the goal of beaming our reports by satellite onto the Internet for the participating schools. Transmissions were also directed to Brussels, Belgium for inclusion in a G-7 Ministerial Conference on the burgeoning Information Highway.

The child encounters were gratifying and a lot of fun but we ended up using the back-up to the back-up plan on all but one occasion to transmit the reports. The satellite up-link equipment was quarters to a brigade of gremlins and even when we managed to lock onto the proper satellite, we played roulette with a file of access codes that rarely worked. The modems wouldn't modem, the computer programs wouldn't compute and then an inverter blew, turning the techno-wizardry into techno-nightmare. We resorted to plugging a portable printer purchased from a taxi driver into the Blazer's cigarette lighter receptacle to print a copy of the report that was then faxed to our office in Canada for insertion on the appropriate Internet web sites.

After 2 weeks on the road, we returned to Istanbul and bid farewell to the GlobaLearn people who flew back to the United States. Jerry and I dropped by a couple of rug shops to say *Allahismarladik* to our favorite sales consultants. They were of course impressed by our *hayirs, yavets* and especially by our proficiency with the good-bye word.

The next day I dropped Jerry at the airport for his flight back to Toronto then inched my way out of Istanbul's gridlock towards the Greek border. No sweat - get out of Turkey, head across Greece to good old Igoumenitsa,

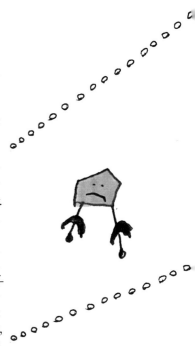

At the inception of mobile satellite communications technology, glitches and gremlins were more likely than a successful transmission.

jump the late light truckers' ferry to Italy and high tail it up the autostrada to Germany. I'd be in Frankfurt in a couple of days.

But with only 50 kilometres of Turkey remaining, the inevitable happened. I crested a hill and there he was, one of Turkey's finest waving me over. The crisply dressed officer gave me a stern look as he drew pictures in his notebook of a Blazer passing a Toyota on a solid line.

"Yavet," I remembered the broken-down Toyota and crossing a double line to get around it.

"Hayir," I won't do it again.

"Money?" Here. How about a half million Turkish lirasi. Fresh new bill I got here, Buddy. More *hayirs* and *yavet*s as my new friend slid the bank note into his pocket. He smiled and nodded in the direction of the Greek border.

I looked him in the eye and gave him my best *Allahaismarladik*. He grinned and shook my hand.

Then I motored west into the sunset trying to wipe the smirk off my face before hitting the Greek border.

"Money?" Here. How about a half million Turkish lirasi. Fresh new bill I got here, Buddy.

6. How Barbie Got Us Home for Christmas

"Flitwick Manor! It's the most haunted hotel in England. People run screaming from there at all hours of the night!" I distinctly remembered those words of warning as the first hints of dawn filtered through the lace curtains.

But something was different. For starters, there was no crick in my neck, no perpetual rocking and I could stretch my legs out. I didn't have boots on and there was no engine drone. All I could hear was the cackling of blackbirds drifting in the open window and the faint sound of a piano playing a Chopin prélude. The smell of clean sheets and the softness of a feather pillow enhanced my confusion.

"Would you like your coffee and toast now?" The voice was muffled, but polite and sweet as she tapped on the door. Not the usual - "It's yer turn. Fuel is at half, not much traffic but lots of caribou. Road's icy in places".

Then again the sweet voice, "Mr. Sowerby, your coffee."

I was foggy-headed that December morning in 1997, but it soon hit me and I laughed out loud. It was over. The day before, Graham McGaw, Colin Bryant and I had finished our around-the-world drive. We had logged in at the zero degree Meridian Line in Greenwich, England with a record time of 21 days 2 hours and 14 minutes, even faster than my deep-down goal of 23 days. We were all delighted with ourselves and the Vauxhall Frontera sport utility truck that had carried us through the 29,000-kilometre driving ordeal.

The anatomically-correct Barbie wreaked havoc on our travel plans.

To top it off, I would soon be hopping a plane to Canada for Christmas. Although, for a while, Christmas at home with my family had seemed unlikely when our Frontera had gone missing during the air freight sector from Auckland, New Zealand to Anchorage, Alaska.

I had flown ahead on a commercial airliner to make arrangements for the North American leg of the trip. On the day the truck was scheduled to arrive, my partners and I dutifully went to the Polar Air cargo terminal to clear the truck through United States Customs. I noted the registration number on the tail of the white Boeing 747 air freighter sitting on the tarmac was the same as the aircraft I had put the Frontera on three days earlier in Auckland.

But, after watching dozens of cargo pallets come off the aircraft, the cargo doors closed and the lumbering jumbo jet taxied to the runway and took off for New York. No Frontera. My partners were ready to mutiny and hop the first flight back to their homes in England.

The cargo agent later told us that our vehicle had been bumped for another shipment and was presently in a storage hangar at the airport in Taipei, Taiwan of all places. This was not good news. The weather was closing in, Christmas was just around the corner and we still had another 9 days of driving, including an airlift from New York to Madrid, before finishing up in London.

Back at the hotel in Anchorage, I tried to determine a course of action that would get us home for Christmas and pacify my restless teammates. I called the cargo manager and asked who was in charge of their operation in the Far East. He provided a cellular phone number for their Vice President who was stuck in traffic in Hong Kong when I reached him. He listened to our problem and promised to call back shortly.

How Barbie Got Us Home for Christmas

"My apologies, but your truck got delayed by a priority shipment of cargo destined for New York. It will arrive in Alaska in 2 or 3 days."

He sounded sincere but our Christmas, along with the logistical and public relations plans for the expedition, was on shaky ground.

I hung up the telephone depressed. Looking for something positive I soon realized that the nature of the priority cargo that had overrode our truck could make the difference. What if it was toys? Toys for Christmas!

I called the Vice President, who was still gridlocked in Hong Kong.

"What was in that cargo shipment that out-ranked our Frontera?" I asked optimistically.

"Ohhhh. Those new anatomically-correct Barbie Dolls. They're selling like crazy in the U.S. and all the stores are short!" He managed a half laugh.

Luck was with us. I wrote a press release titled Barbie Bumps Around-the-World Record Drivers and sent it off to the British public relations firm that had worked itself into a state over the Frontera-in-Taipei predicament.

The British tabloids had a ball with the story. Polar Air managed to re-route the Frontera to Alaska through Australia and get us back on track for the rest of the record attempt, putting us in London two days ahead of our projections. Barbie had saved the day and I would make it home for Christmas.

But what about the sweet voice out in the hall at the haunted Flitwick Manor? The coffee? The toast? I slipped out from under the goose-down duvet and wobbled to the door. Out in the hall lay a tray with a steaming pot of coffee, toast, homemade jam, a silk napkin.

No one was about. Only the sound of someone on the ivories playing Chopin. Somewhere down the hall.

Barbie perhaps.

Flitwick Manor: the most luxuriously accomodating haunted hotel in England.

7. *Taking the High Road*

The motel wasn't much – a strip of rooms with a dirt parking lot handy the airport. There were no screens on the windows and the stained interior walls were in dire need of paint. It was the sort of motel room you're happy to share with someone to help keep an eye out for whatever might creep or slither on by.

Between the stifling heat and noisy aircraft, I didn't get much sleep. Neither did Ken Langley, my partner on that around-the-world record drive attempt back in 1980. After an arduous 12-day drive across India and Pakistan, we were filthy, bug-bitten, exhausted and sick with dysentery. We were also keen to get airlifted out of Pakistan and, with the Karachi airport in sight, we could smell our escape.

The original objective had been to drive east out of Pakistan to Afghanistan through the Khyber Pass then cross Iran and Turkey into Europe. But during our transit of India, the Iran-Iraq war had broken out, terminating that plan.

With the then-Soviet Union out of the question, the only option was to find someone to airlift us over the war. We would make up the lost driving miles required for the record by doing a northern loop into the Scandinavian Arctic. Through our office in Toronto, we managed to convince Lufthansa Airlines to re-route one of its cargo planes, returning to Germany with a load of Bangladeshi carpets, into Pakistan to pick us up. They would drop us and our 1980 Volvo DL station wagon in Athens, circumventing the war.

The Volvo shared cargo space with a load of Bangladeshi carpets in the Boeing 707 that carried us over the Iran-Iraq war.

We got to the Karachi cargo terminal early and started the paperwork to let us and our Nova Scotia-plated car fly off to Greece. Since Ken and I would be traveling on an aircraft configured strictly for freight, additional documentation was required for us to exit Pakistan as 'special couriers'.

The 'what if's' disappeared about noon when the bright orange Boeing 707 taxied up to the hangar. I felt like our mothers were coming to make the nausea go away and airlift us to a playground closer to home.

The German pilots, in a hurry to get back to Frankfurt for happy hour, looked remarkably tidy in the shabby cargo office.

"How vill you be paying for zis?" the Captain, a burly man with a handlebar moustache, asked.

I fumbled for my wallet and pulled out my American Express card.

"Aaah, zat will be fine," he offered, then asked the office manager to charge $18,000 to my already-warped card.

For the next hour we watched the car being loaded onto the aircraft. It gave the Captain a chance to brief us on emergency procedures to follow in case something went haywire during the flight. Since one of the two 'courier' seats was right beside the entry door, he paid particular attention to its operation.

Once inside, we realized how cramped the flight would be. The Volvo was strapped down in front of the carpets leaving little room between its grill and the back of the cockpit door. In our wobbly, dehydrated state, it seemed an edgy place in which to fly over a war. Ken took the only seat in the cargo hold, just aft of the door, hoping for some sleep. I strapped into a seat at the back of the cockpit with a sprawling view out the windscreen between the pilot and co-pilot. I put on a set of headphones and immediately flashed back to my Canadian Armed Forces days crewing DC-3s around western Canada.

"Is hot and veer heavy, veel need every inch vee can get," the Captain advised the First Officer, after being cleared for take-off.

On the climb out, I could see Karachi fading into the haze with an endless stretch of the Arabian Sea pounding its shoreline. We levelled off at 38,000 feet and flew along the south coast of Iran. Later, I saw the heavy, black smoke from the Abadan oil refinery drifting up into the stratosphere. The refinery had been attacked by Iraq a few days earlier and the fire had not yet been brought under control.

The Volvo's license plate stated our goal to drive around the world in 77 days.

Although still sick, I was preoccupied with the view, the chatter from our Abu Dhabi-based air traffic controllers and the operation of the Boeing 707 aircraft. Then Ken tapped me on the shoulder. He looked pale, scared.

"You gotta club me, Sowerby. Put me out for while. I'm really shaky and it's getting claustrophobic back there." I knew it was serious.

"I've got this fascination with the door," he explained. "Can't get my mind off of it. Whenever I close my eyes to try and sleep all I can hear is that song, *Don't Fence Me In*, sounding like it's coming from a cheap megaphone. I see all my relatives marching around to the beat of it when I look out the window."

This didn't sound good. Ken was obviously concerned about the situation and I wasn't keen to leave him alone back there with *the door*.

I thought about telling the Captain but figured stories about my delirious partner wouldn't be impressive. "Er, excuse me, Captain. Do you have a monkey wrench so I can knock Ken out to curb his fascination with that door you showed us how to operate?"

On the horizon I could faintly make out the mountains of Lebanon. We were following pipelines stretching for hundreds of kilometres across the deserts of Saudi Arabia and I felt that once we reached those mountains we would be back on our side of the world and all would be well.

But what about Kenny? I went back to the cargo area, fished a rope out of the Volvo and tied him to his seat, cowboy style. He was cooperative, but we had to get through a few bouts of the giddies in the process. I covered him up with a blanket so the pilots wouldn't see the rope, then watched him drift off to sleep.

Back in the cockpit, I hoped my knots would hold. We were over Lebanon about to head out over the Mediterranean Sea and I felt proud of what we had accomplished. We were through the difficult part of our attempt to drive around the world in 77 days or less and hopefully, now, our health would improve.

And when we landed and pulled up to the hangar in Athens, perhaps Ken could convince the pilots to let him open *the door*.

From the cockpit, I tracked our path along the Arabian Sea, following the coastline of Iran where black smoke from the Iraqi-bombed Abadan oil refinery filled the sky.

8. *Impersonating an Officer*

I was on cruise control motoring west along the 401 between Toronto and Detroit at a respectable 110 kilometres per hour when I first noticed it. Speeders approaching in the overtaking lane eased off as they came up behind me. They would creep up alongside before accelerating back to a cruising speed that would obviously have been of interest to the Ontario Provincial Police.

I stopped for fuel and a sandwich and, while walking back to the car, realized why speeders were taking such an interest in me. From a distance, the silver 2002 Chevy Impala I was driving had *the look* of an unmarked police cruiser; the kind seasoned speeders keep an eye out for.

In my youth, a retired highway patrol car had been high on my 'most wanted' list. Those mid-sixties Chevys, Fords and Dodges had hot police interceptor engines and, with their small hubcaps and sway bars, the base model units had *the look* down pat.

My travel agent, Catherine Tuck, recently purchased a 1996 Ford Crown Victoria that had been a ghost car for the Royal Canadian Mounted Police. With its stance, dual exhaust and fat tires, the tan sedan reeks of authority. Her husband even installed a radio antenna on the trunk lid to improve on *the look*, rationalizing it would protect Catherine from something out there.

My most memorable incident of mistaken identity occurred in 1984, in Ethiopia of all places. After a harrowing, bandit-infested run through northern Kenya, Tim Cat, an employee of the Ethiopian Tourism Commission, met us at the Ethiopian border town of Moyale.

The gateway into southern Ethiopia, on the northern edge of the Kasuit Desert, had been a thriving village. But when the pro-Soviet-style military government, led by Mengistu Haile Mariam, toppled the Emperor Haile Selassie 10 years earlier, relations with Kenya had deteriorated and the border was closed.

Some diplomatic maneuvering had convinced the Ethiopian government to let us enter the country by road at Moyale if we agreed to participate in a press conference in Addis Ababa, the capital city. Our role would be to extol the virtues of vacationing in Ethiopia. As part of the deal, we agreed to hire a tourism official that would travel with us the entire Ethiopian leg of our trip from South Africa to Norway. I liked the idea of having a local on board and Tim Cat, who seemed to have friends everywhere, turned out to be a valuable asset as we made our way across the parched country.

The thousand-kilometre drive between the border and Addis Ababa took us through the northern part of the Great Rift Valley. Most towns had gates at their entrances where military people examined our papers while Tim Cat enthusiastically explained what we were up to. He described how the bullet holes ended up in the side of our GMC Suburban truck and showed off its then-techie amenities. Good stuff in the fellowship department but not conducive to setting a timed distance driving record.

Nearing Debre Zeyit, two hundred kilometres south of the capital, we

… relations with Kenya had deteriorated and the border was closed.

prepared for the usual drill of producing letters of introduction, passports, insurance papers and the Carnet de Passage, a must-have customs document for the Suburban. A fresh pack of cigarettes was strategically positioned on the dashboard. But as we approached, the gate swung open, the guards snapped to attention, saluted and waved us through. Beyond the gates, the masses lined the streets waving and cheering as we passed. School children, dressed in crisp blue uniforms, waved Ethiopian flags.

"This is unbelievable!" I told Tim Cat, feeling both proud and humbled by the enthusiastic display of emotion from complete strangers.

"I know nothing of this," he laughed, waving to the cheering people as we sped by.

We encountered similar greetings at other towns before rolling into Addis Ababa for the press conference. Thinking the ambush story might clash with our objective to promote Ethiopia as a desirable tourist destination, I parked the truck up against a cement wall, keeping the bullet holes out of sight.

School children greeted us warmly as we drove through the small towns of Ethiopia.

After the conference and a security briefing, we prepared for our departure to Djibouti, 800 kilometres away at the southern end of the Red Sea. Tim Cat looked at me with a mischievous grin.

"You know what was going on in those towns with the big receptions?"

He had talked to one of his colleagues and could hardly wait to get it out.

"What?" I asked, preoccupied that we couldn't find any tires to replace the three spares that had gotten us mobile after the shootout in the Kenyan desert.

"It was the president, Mr. Mengistu. He was due to pass through those places when we came through. Everyone thought we were the official vehicle and I was him." Tim Cat enjoyed telling the story and having had a chance to impersonate the ultimate officer, without even trying.

He went on to explain that, after we passed the masses had dispersed, the children returned to school and the gatekeepers went back to scrutinizing travel documents, throwing a wrench into Mr. Mengistu's propaganda machine.

I was still reliving those memories when I drove the Impala with *the look* across Windsor to the entrance of the tunnel under the Detroit River. At the other end, I pulled up to the U.S. Customs and Immigration booth, but no one waved me through before checking my papers.

The masses weren't lining the streets of Detroit either. And there were no school children waving flags as I passed.

Not one.

Security gates barring the entrance of most Ethiopian towns meant constant document checks on the road.

9. The Coat

The Canada Goose parka was massive. It had dwarfed everything else in the store.

When an opportunity arose for a trip to Tuktoyaktuk, on the shores of the Arctic Ocean, I jumped at the chance. It would give me an occasion to visit one of the most northerly communities on the North American mainland while adding the Northwest Territories to the roster of places I have visited.

It would also offer the chance to drive the 190-kilometre ice road that connects Tuktoyaktuk with Inuvik during the winter months. The ice road meanders on the frozen waterways of the Mackenzie River Delta then parallels the coast of the Arctic Ocean before reaching Tuktoyaktuk.

The week before leaving, Lisa monitored Inuvik weather on the internet and confirmed temperatures hovering in the –40 degrees Celsius range.

The sun rose at 11:23 and set at 4:51 in the afternoon.

"What will we wear?" Her question was logical as she rummaged through the clothing I wore to Alaska in 1987. I finally admitted the clothing now fit her better, leaving me out in the cold in the wardrobe department.

I remembered an Arctic expedition parka that my good friend Jon Clark had at his store, The Trail Shop, in Halifax, Nova Scotia. I had eyed it last fall, wondering who would ever need such a garment.

The Canada Goose parka was massive. It had dwarfed everything else in the store and I suspected that, if Jon still had it, he would be ready to cut a deal on the navy blue, down-filled, canvas unit with a coyote fur-trimmed hood.

I went to The Trail Shop and tried it on. Jon helped me adjust a series of draw strings, Velcro fasteners and zippers. When I put the hood up, my head disappeared into a cavern. Voices became muted. I peered out of the giant fur-lined pea shooter as Jon mouthed something about handling anything the Arctic could throw at me.

"But it's almost $500 and I'll probably never get a chance to wear it again after Tuktoyaktuk." I felt like a winter version of the Michelin man.

"I'll give you a great deal. Make sure to wear the hood half down like this so the locals don't suspect you're from the South," Jon advised, before yanking it backwards then ruffling it up against the back of my head.

The coyote fur tickled my ears. I checked my look in the mirror and saw someone ready to take on the Yukon Quest sled dog race.

It wasn't until I got home that I realized there was only one way to get The Coat up to Inuvik for the ice road drive to Tuktoyaktuk. Wear it.

Lisa looked like a stick person walking through the Halifax airport beside me. We managed an upgrade to Business Class and when I asked the flight attendant if she could hang up my coat, she backed away, saying it would fill the closet. It felt like I was stuffing a walrus into the overhead compartment. I could feel everyone's eyes on me. Did *the suits* think they had a brave Arctic explorer in their midst, or a climatically dysfunctional moron?

We overnighted in Vancouver, where the doorman at the Bayshore Inn gave me wide berth. In the morning, we approached the Air Canada ticket counter for our flight to Whitchorse, Yukon Territory.

… my head disappeared into a cavern. Voices became muted.

"Going south, I see." The tanned ticket agent couldn't resist.

In Whitehorse, Lisa got started with the rental car clerk while I went for the bags. She told him I would be there shortly with my driver's licence.

"Is that him in The Coat?" He grinned. Lisa didn't have to look to confirm.

On the way to the hotel, Lisa told me that wearing the hood half up gave me a bad case of Hood Head. This close relative of bed head made my profile resemble an anvil, not exactly the intrepid Arctic explorer look.

That night I sat The Coat up in an arm chair then put the hood up and stuffed it with newspaper. It felt like we had a visiting relative along, always there in the periphery. A quiet, noble presence.

Landing in Inuvik the next day, I finally fit in. In the streets of this lively Arctic outpost at the end of the Dempster Highway, Lisa pointed out a couple of different versions of my Canada Goose parka. I wanted to waddle over and talk to them, see if they had any advice for Hood Head. Did it affect their social lives? Was advanced Hood Head a status symbol?

In the morning we left Inuvik, driving up the East Channel of the MacKenzie River. The plowed ice road was much wider than I had imagined, like an eight-lane highway in places. We drove our rented GMC Jimmy between 50 and 85 kilometres per hour most of the time, slower on the corners. The leisurely Arctic sunrise played out a spectacular display of pastel colours on cloudbanks hanging over patches of ice fog. On the greenish-grey sea ice, we encountered ominous signs, warning of cracks ahead.

In Tuk, we ventured into the only hotel, the Tuk Inn. I propped The Coat on a chair in the modest dining room and ordered chicken soup and Eskimo doughnuts, a local specialty of deep-fried bread dough. It was an intimate scene, just Lisa and I up there at what seemed like the top of the

The only hotel in Tuktoyaktuk offered a cozy respite from the Arctic chill at the top of the world.

planet. The Coat hunched over the chair beside us like a sentry ready to protect us from the northern elements.

Halfway through lunch, the local wildlife officer dropped in. His wife ran the hotel and they talked about chores their kids would do after school. On the way out, he stopped by our table.

"So it's you two!" I noticed his light windbreaker with a Government of Canada logo on it. "You brought this lovely spring weather."

"Only twenty below today," he grinned, eyeing The Coat. "Last week it was minus fifty with the wind chill."

I thought about the long trip back home to Halifax. Hood Head would ride again.

Chapter 2 *Revving Up*

The rocker panels had all but disintegrated and a hole in the floor had grown to a point where small grocery items, like a box of Kraft dinner or a pack of baloney, would drop onto the pavement below.

10. Sultry Cheryl and the Swollen Thumb

During the summer of 1967, the Boy Scouts invited me to work in Montreal at Expo '67, the World's Fair celebrating the 100th year of Canadian confederation. My job was stamping passports at the Ethiopian pavilion.

One afternoon, two ravishing girls came by and I dutifully entered the Ethiopian seal into their passports.

"Where y'all from?" Her voice made my knees buckle. She thought I was Ethiopian and was surprised when I told her the garb I was wearing was a Boy Scout uniform. Her name was Cheryl. She was from Atlanta, Georgia.

When my shift ended, Cheryl was out front waiting. We strolled through the Expo '67 complex. She was 19. I was 16, but told her I was 18.

We gazed into each other's eyes every afternoon until she left for Atlanta a few days later. After my stint at the Ethiopian pavilion, I took the train back home to Moncton, New Brunswick. All I could think about was Cheryl.

Her friend stifled a giggle as I lugged Mum's Samsonite suitcase out of the airport and placed it into the trunk of a new red Cadillac convertible.

I wrote her every second day during grade 12, about 150 letters, and she wrote back almost as many. We planned on seeing each other the next summer after I finished high school.

I decided to call her one February evening, but didn't want my parents to know. So I went to a local telephone booth with five dollars in quarters, enough for about four minutes. I listened to Cheryl's sultry southern drawl for an eternity before hanging up. The payphone immediately rang so I answered, thinking it might somehow be Cheryl, but it was the operator demanding forty dollars in overtime charges.

"Forty dollars!" I told her I had to wash 133 cars at my part-time job for that kind of money. She was sympathetic but warned if I didn't pay, they would charge Cheryl's number. With an hour's reprieve, I scraped up the money then dropped 160 quarters into the payphone.

That summer, I washed cars at the dealership, daydreaming about Cheryl most of the time. I promised her that if I got an entry scholarship for university, I'd visit her in Atlanta, so when the scholarship materialized, I called with the news.

I still can't believe my parents let me go. I was 17, had only been on an airplane once, and had never travelled to the United States.

"You're not going there looking like some kind of a hick." From Mum's tone I knew wherever she was headed, I would oblige. "You're wearing a suit on that airplane."

So, like an imbecile, I wore my Sunday best on the overnight flight to Atlanta. My outfit consisted of a black miracle-fibre suit, a white shirt and a thin black tie with a shimmering green stripe down the centre. A pair of hopelessly pointed fake alligator shoes complemented the ensemble. I looked like a cross between Jerry Lee Lewis and Liberace.

I spent the night talking to everyone on the airplane. Before meeting Cheryl at the Atlanta airport, I went into the washroom, filled the sink with water, and plunged my head into it. After drying my hair with paper towels, I slicked everything back into a ducktail with a high frontal wave à la Troy Donahue.

Cheryl was waiting by the baggage claim. She was more beautiful than I remembered and had an equally stunning girlfriend in tow. Two drops of water trickled from my hair into my left eye. I suppose they thought I was crying. Her friend stifled a giggle as I lugged Mum's Samsonite suitcase

My job was stamping passports at the Ethiopian pavilion.

out of the airport and placed it into the trunk of a new red Cadillac convertible. I had never been in a Cadillac and made sure to tell them.

"Why don't we stop and get something to eat?" Cheryl suggested, as I soaked up Atlanta from the back seat of the Caddy.

At the restaurant, I didn't understand much of the menu and ordered what Cheryl did. I told them most cars in Moncton did not have air conditioners and that the Pontiacs sold in the U.S. had different suspensions than the ones sold in Canada. They didn't seem excited that my dad's new pick-up truck was one of the few in Moncton with the optional 352-cubic inch V-8 engine.

Dinner dates back home didn't amount to more than a couple of plates of French fries with gravy, and a bill over a few dollars was considered hefty. So when the $56.00 tab came, parting with half of my spending money for the week was a real shocker.

At Cheryl's house, I met Mother. Daddy was away on business. Cheryl invited me into the backyard and, after I commented on never having been at a house with a swimming pool, advised me she had to go out and wouldn't return until midnight.

I smelled a rat. And when she told me she was meeting the guy she was about to marry, I tasted one.

"But y'all can borrow Mother's car and go for a drive." I thought about the flashy Cadillac ragtop and cheered up. After she left, Mother told me her car was in the garage, in front of the Caddy. The blue 1964 Ford Falcon didn't even have whitewall tires.

I cruised around in the Falcon, rubber-necking at a world I had only ever imagined. When I got hungry, I stopped by a Kentucky Fried Chicken and brought the booty back to Cheryl's house.

Getting out of the car, I slammed the door on my thumb and it swelled to twice its normal size. That evening, I watched colour TV for the first time. Her mother and I chatted during commercials, mostly about plans for the upcoming wedding.

Two days later, Cheryl drove me to the airport in the red Cadillac. We didn't talk much. My slicked-back hair was blowing in the wind. My thumb was throbbing.

The miracle-fibre suit and the fake alligator shoes were in the back seat, stuffed into Mum's Samsonite suitcase.

So, like an imbecile, I wore my Sunday best on the overnight flight to Atlanta.

11. Cool College Cars

Aside from a ninety-dollar 1954 Ford Victoria I bought the last year of high school, my first ventures into vehicular ownership were at college. Yes, my time at Sackville, New Brunswick's Mount Allison University between 1968 and 1972 provided the chance to dabble with more cars than was probably necessary.

My identical twin brother Larry was attending Mount Allison at the same time so we decided to go splits on any vehicles we bought. If we had more than one, then I owned half of each of them. The concept of splitting ownership on more than one car seemed rather exotic with its option to change units daily. It also meant paying half the repair bills on twice as many cars, which was akin to pooling lottery tickets where you

It was a red-roofed, monochromatic masterpiece topped off with a 2x10-inch plank bolted to the front for a bumper.

have 10 times the chance to win a tenth of the prize.

We arrived at Mount Allison in a '61 Mercury Monterey that we bought for $600. The immaculate gunmetal grey beauty had originally belonged to my father. We picked it up after the second owner traded it at the car dealership where we had part-time jobs as car cleaners and lot boys. Six years earlier, as a twelve-year-old, I had learned to detail cars to full nerd level on that Mercury. I steel-wooled the white wall tires, spent hours getting at interior bits with a toothbrush and kept the engine so spotless it looked like an autoshow display.

The next summer, between freshman and sophomore years, we sold the Monterey for $1,000 to use toward the purchase of a two-year-old 1967 Mustang Fastback. The GT 390 four-speed manual, sporting 335 horsepower and 4:11 gears, is still a favorite of the 60 or so cars I have owned.

Between freshman and sophomore years we sold the Monterey for $1,000 to use toward the purchase of a two-year-old 1967 Mustang Fastback.

The Mustang was a great ride but all those horses and the wide oval tires were not conducive to driving in the harsh winters on the Tantramar Marshes that separated New Brunswick from Nova Scotia. So the Mustang went into storage while Larry and I went in search of a winter drift-jumper.

We found it on Thanksgiving weekend during a visit home for the turkey feed. Larry spotted a car that belonged to Ralph Whitely, our grade 8 science teacher, with a *For Sale* sign on it. The 1961 Vauxhall Victor was at the absolute other end of the cool spectrum from the flashy Mustang. Mr. Whitely had put rear leaf springs from a '58 Ford on the faded gold heap which jacked the rear an extra foot into the air. With plenty of rust and the skinniest tires we had ever seen, it was butt ugly.

Of course we had to have it. We forked over $135 to Mr. Whitely, slapped 'Whose Chicken?' decals on the front quarter panels and headed back to Mount A, feeling somewhat humbled without our rip-snorting red Mustang.

The Vauxhall turned out to be a campus hit as it degenerated through the fall and winter. By February, the rocker panels had all but disintegrated and a hole in the floor had grown to a point where small grocery items, like a box of Kraft dinner or a pack of baloney, would drop onto the pavement below. One of the rear spring shackles got into the habit of flipping itself around throwing the right rear of the body so high into the air that the left front bumper would scrape on the pavement. No problem, we just removed the bumper and stuffed it under Larry's bed. Ugly was getting reallllly ugly!

But the Vauxhall never needed work other than the engine block heater Don Filmore, the mechanic at the local Irving filling station, installed for the icy winter nights. The heater, from a 389 Pontiac GTO, kept the little 4-cylinder so warm that, even on mornings when the temperature plunged to minus 30 degrees Celsius, using the manual choke would flood the carburetor.

One day Don told me that New Brunswick was introducing a safety inspection sticker system and the Vauxhall would need one because the town cops had their eye on it. Don knew that mechanically it was OK but told me I had to put rocker panels and a bumper on it. He thought a paint job wouldn't hurt either.

I sacrificed the next weekend to work on the Vauxhall. The paint shop at the local Mercury Lincoln dealership gave me the dregs of a half dozen cans of paint. I mixed the contents together resulting in a light florescent green colour that looked like bad-tasting medicine.

I bought galvanized eavestroughs and pot-riveted them into the place of rocker panels. Duct tape was used to cover most of the rust holes and then I hand brushed the gooey green mixture onto it from the bottom up. That way if I ran out of paint the worst of the lower body rust would be covered up.

I didn't have enough for the roof so I painted it with red primer while everything but the glass, tires and lights got the green slime. It was a red-

The Mustang that I co-owned with twin brother Larry, has always been a long-standing favourite.

roofed, monochromatic masterpiece topped off with a 2x10-inch plank bolted to the front for a bumper. Clearance lights from a transport truck were attached to the top of the front fenders for turn signals. A circuit connector switch 'borrowed' from a physics lab was bolted to the dash as a horn button and we soon became adept at slapping the dashboard whenever a blow of the horn was necessary. Problem was that I slapped the dash on everything I drove after that looking for the horn, even my dad's snazzy new Thunderbird.

In the spring we got the Mustang out of storage. The Vauxhall had done its job so it went up for sale. A young farmer from Rockport, a 5-house community at the head of the Bay of Fundy, bought it for $90. His wife was in the last stages of pregnancy and he needed a car to get her to the hospital when the time came. We showed him the quick-draw horn button, how to flip the errant spring shackle back into position and warned him about not choking it when the block heater was used.

The following Fall we put the Mustang away and picked up another Vauxhall Victor, but this one was in pristine shape. One afternoon I took a drive to Rockport to look for the Green Slime.

It wasn't in the driveway of the man we sold it to but in the cornfield across the street I noticed an odd-looking rudimentary farm tractor. It was hooked up to a small utility trailer, had very skinny front tires and the back was jacked up to the point of ridiculousness.

Then I noticed the front bumper. It was made of wood and, although badly splintered and scratched, the fluorescent green colour was unmistakable.

The 1961 Vauxhall Victor was at the absolute other end of the cool spectrum from the flashy Mustang.

12. *There's Gold in that Logo*

When Ken Langley and I decided to quit our jobs and raise a quarter of a million dollars to set a new around-the-world driving record, we realized it was risky business. Paycheques, job security and our cushy offices would become a thing of the past. And there were no guarantees our venture would ever get to the start line, let alone propel us around the world in record time.

Before approaching an organization for sponsorship, we would need a plan, a sales package and a way to convince the corporate world that our idea was a savvy way to meet their business goals. Once they bought into the idea, we still had to convince them that we were the guys to do it.

Garry Sowerby
Odyssey International Ltd.
P.O. Box 22-177 • Bayers Road RPO • Halifax • Nova Scotia • Canada • B3L 4T7
Tel: 902.455.8258 • Fax: 902.455.9557 • Cell: 902.452.3177
email: odyssey@hfx.eastlink.ca • www.adventuredrive.ca

We figured sponsors would rather deal with another corporate identity than a couple of nobodies from Nova Scotia, so our first step was to incorporate Odyssey International Limited. We sold shares to 49 investors, a gaggle of friends and relatives. The $25,000 seed money would be used to finance our research, to develop a sales package and for travel expenses to meet with potential sponsors. It would also be used to commission an artist who would develop a key ingredient of Odyssey's image; our logo.

We incorporated Odyssey International Limited on February 15, 1979 at Halifax's venerable City Club amid a gathering of shareholders and business associates. It was a celebratory affair. We drank cocktails, feasted on Beef Wellington and charmed our guests. After dinner, we sipped fine cognac while signing incorporation papers in a haze of cigar smoke and dreams of grandeur.

The next morning, I went to the second floor of The Green Lantern Building where we shared a suite of offices with our lawyer, Tom Khattar, who was inaugurating his law practice the same day. My first meeting was with a graphic artist who was coming over at 9:30 to present a logo concept. Feeling a tad seedy from incorporation night festivities, I advised our receptionist I would be taking a nap and to make sure she roused me before letting the visitor into my office.

I laid down on the purple shag carpet behind my desk, covered up in my sports jacket and drifted off. Of course, our receptionist was out for coffee when the artist arrived, so he nosed his way into my chambers.

"Ahh, errr, I was just getting a little rest," I mumbled, rubbing bloodshot eyes. My necktie was choking. My matted hair felt like a Brillo pad.

I was thinking about the throbbing in my temples as he unveiled his logo rendition with the word *Odyssey* above *International Limited* in a smaller font. The 'O' in Odyssey had been filled in with a map of the world representing our challenge to conquer the planet.

"Good concept," I thought. But the more I looked at it, the more I saw a globe in front of 'dyssey International Limited'. Or was it more how I

But the more I looked at it, the more I saw a globe in front of 'dyssey International Limited'. Or was it more how I felt at the time… 'dizzy International Limited'?

felt at the time… 'dizzy International Limited'?

Ken and I presented the artwork to our board of directors who all agreed that 'Dizzy International' was not the way to go. The next day, I met with a young artist who had a studio one floor up from our office at the Green Lantern. She assured me that our logo problem could be solved in a few days for $50.

Meanwhile, Ken and I lined up a series of meetings in Toronto and bought a 1962 black Ford Thunderbird for $1,500 to make the trip. It was in fabulous shape. We planned on selling it in Toronto for $3,000 and using the profit to pay for the trip, a prudent business maneuver of which our shareholders and directors would obviously be proud.

On the eve of our departure, I met with the artist. Since time was tight and I still had to road-test the T-Bird for the Toronto trek, I asked if she wanted to talk logo while I checked out the road manners of our investment on a 100-kilometre driving loop.

She showed me her concept, simply an arrow made up of five smaller blue arrows. She was clearly pleased with her work, and I liked it too.

"When we break the around-the-world record, we'll make one of the arrows gold," I suggested, feeling somewhat concerned that the T-Bird was constantly drifting to the right.

By the time we started back for Halifax, logo talk had evolved into a

Fine cognac and Cuban cigars at Halifax's City Club provided the backdrop as founding directors, Larry Sowerby (left), Tom Khattar (hidden), Ken Langley (centre), Garry Sowerby and Larry Hood (far right), signed incorporation documents.

career concept. Odyssey would go on to set more world records, making another arrow gold after each accomplishment. When there were 5 gold arrows, I would retire.

Back in Halifax, the drift to the right had been eclipsed by dreams of gold arrow evolution. Then, a block from the City Club, at precisely the time I asked her to apply the artwork to our much-awaited letterhead, the right front tire exploded. The brake had been dragging, overheating the brake drum causing the tire to blow. The force of the blowout ruptured the brake line which spewed brake fluid on the overheated assembly.

A fire broke out and within minutes police and fire trucks were on the scene. The front end of the T-Bird was toast so I sold it to the wrecking company for $500 terminating plans for a profitable sales trip to Toronto.

But I've used the logo ever since. The one on the Volvo we ended up racing around the world in 1980 has one gold arrow, our Africa-Arctic Suburban has two and the GMC Sierra Tim Cahill and I drove from the bottom to the top of the Americas has three. In a museum in England, the Vauxhall Frontera with which I set another around-the-world record has four gold arrows in its logo. And so does the latest version of our business card and letterhead.

But there is still one more gold to go. And every now and then, I scratch my greying head and wonder.

A gold arrow in our logo signifies a new world driving record. With five arrows to turn from blue to gold, we knew it would be a long road ahead.

13. *Just the Grey Flannels, Please!*

I usually do the 400-kilometre drive between Toronto and Detroit in one shot; four hours of cruise control wrestling ideas I'm about to lay on an automotive executive in Motor City. On a recent trip, I realized the ritual has been going on for 20 years.

My ride on that first trip offered few of the amenities found aboard the Northstar V-8-endowed Caddy DeVille in which I was presently nestled. The propane-powered 1982 Checker taxicab I had purchased from the Checker Motor Company in Kalamazoo, Michigan to enter in the Peking-Paris Motoring Challenge, epitomized basic. Not even a radio.

The British-based Peking-Paris promoter never got the event off the ground so I was drumming up sponsorship for an attempt at the speed record for the fastest drive from the South Cape of Africa to the North Cape of Europe. I had been hopelessly flogging the idea to corporate

I kept an eye out for stores that would obviously be flooded with 'grey flannels' for under $38.00 which was precisely what I had in the pocket of my faded blue jeans.

Toronto for months and, with a banker threatening to force us into bankruptcy, the dream was on the line.

In a final move of desperation, I scored a 15-minute audience with John Rock, General Manager of GMC Truck Division in Pontiac, Michigan, then convinced the bank manager to hold off until after the meeting. Before leaving Toronto, while anticipating Mr. Rock's probable questions, I realized my only business suit was among the missing.

The last time I remembered seeing it was in a motel in Des Moines, Iowa draped over a turquoise leatherette armchair. A frenzied search of my closet turned up a double-breasted navy blazer, appropriate white shirt and a maroon tie that Guinness Superlatives had bestowed upon me after setting the around-the-world driving record that had created the financial mess from which I was hoping the suit would extricate me.

The propane-powered taxicab was the last one sold by the Checker Motor Company in Kalamazoo, Michigan.

I borrowed $150 from Paul Solomons, a crony who had that much faith in my ability to pull a GMC Suburban out of the hat for our second world driving record attempt. Paul's loan would fill the Checker with enough propane to get me to Michigan and back across the border to Windsor. A night's lodging and a few sandwiches would leave about $35 to purchase a pair of grey flannel pants that would nicely complement the blazer/Guinness tie combo.

I motored to Windsor the night before the meeting and checked into a budget motel with a lumpy bed. In the morning I would cross the border, drive the 80 kilometres to Mr. Rock's office in Pontiac and still have plenty of time to find appropriate pantwear before the one o'clock meeting. I went to sleep biled-up realizing that if I blew the meeting, or if John Rock didn't like me or the Africa-Arctic idea, it would be the end of the fascinating tangent my life had taken when I decided to drive a car around the world five years earlier.

The border was a snap and I maneuvered the lumbering Checker through the labyrinth of highways across Detroit like a seasoned cabby. I kept an eye out for stores that would obviously be flooded with 'grey flannels' for under $38.00 which was precisely what I had in the pocket of my faded blue jeans.

Over the next 3 hours I rummaged through a dozen stores, many with the perfect pant in the $70 –100 range. But with no credit cards, all I could do was panic. By noon I had worked my way into Pontiac and could

I scored a 15-minute audience with John Rock, General Manager of GMC Truck Division in Pontiac, Michigan.

see the Phoenix Center, home of GMC Truck where Mr. Rock would take one look at my blue blazer/faded jean ensemble and splatter the Africa-Arctic dream like one of the flies in the grill of the Checker.

By 12:30, while frantically considering calling John Rock with a lame excuse about being held up at the border, I spotted a 'Jeans 'n Things' store in a strip mall a few blocks from the Phoenix Center. I wiped the sweat from my forehead and went in.

"'Ey mon, like that car." The lone sales clerk looked like he meant it.

"It's the last one off the assembly line. I bought it to drive in a race across China that never happened," I volunteered. "But what about a pair of grey flannels?"

"Oh mon, nothing like that here." He kept eyeing the Checker.

I went on about world driving records, my proposal to Mr. Big at the GMC palace down the street, the banker in Toronto with a dripping pen about to shut me down and the $38 in my pocket.

"You must have something that would resemble grey flannels from a distance?" I figured I'd talk a lot and keep John Rock from dwelling on my pantwear.

The clerk went to the back of the store reappearing with a polyester pair of grey slacks that looked like something an ESSO Home Comfort burner repairman would wear to an after-hours house call.

"They're $59.95, mon. But for you, today - half price. And my mother can be here in five minutes to hem them." He looked as excited as I was. His mother hemmed them right around my bony ankles and I fled for the meeting.

I found my way to Mr. Rock's office without a spare second to hatch any pre-presentation jitters. As I sat down across his massive desk, the knife-edge crease in those miracle-fibre flannels glistened in my peripheral vision.

The 15-minute meeting stretched into a two-hour session. I liked his easy-going manner and he appreciated the Africa-Arctic idea as well as another dozen or so driving adventures we subsequently dreamed up before his retirement on January 1, 1997.

And I often wonder, if that guy in the "Jeans 'n Things" store hadn't been who he was or if I hadn't been so distracted by pant panic, whether that first meeting with John Rock might have resulted in a polite 15-minute brush off.

14. Car Fever

It can strike anytime but most cases develop in the spring. Although I have never seen statistics, I suspect it affects more males than females, usually lasting a day or two. But the affliction has been known to go on for weeks and in some low-grade cases, for years.

Symptoms include insomnia, difficulty concentrating, communication lapses, bouts of euphoria and periods of procrastination with respect to family and vocational responsibilities. Although deemed a fever, there is usually no elevation of body temperature associated with the condition that can stretch relationships to their elastic limit.

Car fever, that obsessive crave for a new set of wheels, infiltrates everyday life with the pervasiveness and tenacity of a well-hacked computer virus.

Early on, my father showed me many fine examples. In the late '50s and '60s, he went on annual buying rampages that put our family into a string of Buicks and Mercurys. Those Detroit beauties, along with the two trucks he used in his plate glass business, defined the landscape of our comfortable home in the north end of Moncton, New Brunswick. Lee Sowerby's fleet was new, detailed and usually had the biggest engines available. His vehicular realm was a fertile breeding ground for car fever.

My father's immaculate fleet of Detroit beauties were the envy of the neighborhood.

"Where's Dad?" twin brother Larry or I would want to know when he was late for dinner.

"He's down at Steeves Motors again." Mum was resigned to being a single parent for the next few days while good old Dad was at the Pontiac-Buick-Cadillac dealership hammering out a deal.

In my eight-year-old mind's eye, I could see him in a small room with two or three car salesmen slamming fists on the table over a hundred dollars. Big time stuff. Dad would, of course, stomp out and have to be coaxed back in. More fists slamming on the desk.

Finally, on the third night he walks in with that familiar grin. Outside is a cream 1958 Buick Special. We'd seen it many times in preceding weeks from the back seat of our 14-month-old '57 Buick hardtop, cruising the Steeves Motors lot with Dad while our unsuspecting mother was home doing the dinner dishes.

Over the next 10 years he went through a parade of Mercury Montereys and Park Lanes, even a suicide-door Thunderbird when I was a senior in high school. By then both Larry and I had begun a continuous cycle of vehicle purchases that has left both of us with stables of cars and trucks that are, by some standards, out of control.

Dad's glass truck was the worker among the string of shiny new Buicks and Mercurys that paraded through my childhood.

My father's haggling at the local car dealerships got us our first job, washing cars at the Lincoln Mercury shop. We would keep on top of the 75- to 100-unit lot for 25 cents a car, which we split. Not bad for a couple of 13-year-olds. Our after school and weekend job was a good place to await delivery of a 1966 Mercury half-ton pick-up that Dad had ordered. The silver-grey beauty had a 220 horse, 352 cubic inch V8 engine, a three-in-the-tree column shifter and the optional full-length bodyside moulding.

But there was a downside to car fever. When the "new wheels" hoopla died down, I was haunted by a lingering emptiness without the old car Dad had traded in. After all, they were perfectly maintained cars that Larry and I had fussed over during their life in the Sowerby driveway. I learned to drive in them. I had my first dates in them. There was always the chance of seeing the new owner driving around with scraped whitewalls. I hated the idea of seeing it being neglected. No more waxed valve covers.

Symptoms include insomnia, difficulty concentrating, communication lapses, bouts of euphoria…

I used to dream about what it would be like to keep all the cars you ever owned. The millstone of an ever-growing fleet would carry weight in the decision to purchase a new car. The added baggage of insurance, maintenance, licence and storage would have to be considered. I figured that after a few cars the concept would abate my fever for new wheels.

I started about 15 years ago and now have 11 cars and trucks. There is always a leased unit that my wife Lisa drives. The other ten are my problems. That's 40 tires to replace, ten dipsticks to check, a fleet insurance policy and a storage facility for up to 10 cars where I can hide and nerd out to my heart's content. The change-up of driving a different one every few weeks keeps my car fever in check.

Brother Larry has not fared so well, however. With only five in his fleet and no 'can't sell the old one' rule, he drives his wife, family and me batty at times. One day he drops by in a Porsche 911. He waxes on about how he could fall in love with it and keep it forever. A week later he's back showing me a new Suburban, then an eight-year-old BMW 750. He ended up with a speedboat then had to buy a new Chevy Silverado to tow it around. In my opinion, he is in a constant state of car fever.

For me, when the fever hits like it did when I saw the engine in a new Mustang Cobra last month, I ride it out for a few days. Dream the dreams, toss and turn, bore the family till I get down to the compound and check out my fleet.

My parents, Lee and Edith Sowerby, during a period of remission from 'the fever'.

Then, all those tires and dipsticks are usually enough to bring down the fever.

Chapter 3 *Chasing Gremlins*

*W*hen he was excited it got even louder, borderline yelling. Sometimes I'd be up in my bedroom drifting off to sleep and I'd hear it through the floorboards. "Poor car. Poorest car I ever had!"

15. Breathless

There was no doubt about it; I was driving fast along the narrow, twisty secondary road. I had a feeling the ferry might not run after midnight and, considering the circumstances, it was imperative we make it to the boat that would take us across the Kennebecasis River so we could get to Saint John, New Brunswick as quickly as possible.

I eased off, slipping through patches of ground fog, but on the high ground under the yellow cast of a full moon, I hammered the throttle and let the intercooled turbocharged engine do its magic with the agile Subaru Impreza WRX station wagon I was driving. Every now and then, I would catch the faint silhouette of my 15-year-old daughter strapped into the passenger's seat.

"Is it getting worse?" I asked, trying to conceal my concern.

"No, but if it closes up before we get to the hospital what will we do?" She sounded scared, on the verge of crying.

A few hours earlier Natalie had complained of a constriction in her windpipe that seemed to be cutting off her ability to breathe properly. It

The ride in John Paynter's rally-equipped Subaru WRX was a thrill I'll not soon forget.

was a feeling she had never experienced before and, considering we were at old friends Pat and Joe Tippett's cottage on the Saint John River an hour away from any medical help, I decided to take her to the hospital for a professional opinion.

I had heard too many horrific stories about allergic reactions and even though Natalie did not have a history of allergies, I had no idea what she may have encountered during the previous two days of swimming, tubing and romping around the lush vegetation along the river.

I was thankful to be behind the wheel of an exceptionally safe, well-handling car. Maneuvering through the labyrinth of back roads, I thought about the experience two days earlier when I had an opportunity to ride as a passenger with Canadian rally champion John Paynter. With the exception of suspension modifications, a roll cage and a free flow exhaust system his car was essentially the same as the WRX in which I was driving Natalie to the hospital.

The ride with Paynter, down a designated one-lane private logging road, defied what I considered a car could do. He had casually drifted the WRX through impossible corners at ridiculous speeds with the ease most people push shopping carts through Bob Loblaw's grocery stores. Getting airborne on some straight stretch rises added to my wonder of when anyone would ever need a car that could do what his WRX was doing. But now, with the ferry dock in sight, I was using every bit of those performance ingredients to get Natalie to someone who could tell us what was going on in her throat.

Earlier in the week, I had taken my travel agent, Catherine Tuck, on a spin in the WRX. At one point, while waxing on about the car's features, I forced the throttle down in second gear on a highway entrance ramp.

"With 227 turbocharged horsepower, it really hauls. Except for that slight turbo whine there is no engine noise, even under full throttle." The tachometer was approaching the 7200 RPM redline.

Catherine was rigid with feet braced to the floor. Both hands white-knuckled the armrest. Her wide eyes reminded me of a scene from *Night of the Living Dead*. As I slammed the shifter into 3rd gear, I heard her quietly murmur "… no engine noise".

But not as quiet as Natalie and I were during the short ferry ride across the shimmering, moonlit Kennebecasis River. She was obviously upset and I didn't want her to know how worried I was. Then, after making our way through the town of Quispamsis, it was a straight shot down a virtually empty four-laner into Saint John.

At the hospital, we were fast-tracked through the paperwork and taken directly to a treatment room, bypassing the horde of waiting room late-nighters. A doctor was with us shortly, poking and prodding at Natalie while presenting a barrage of questions about allergies and her activities over the previous 24 hours. He looked serious.

Natalie and I took turns explaining what she had been up to … swimming, playing cards, laughing and screaming on the back of a tube towed by a motorboat.

"Lots of that tube-towing stuff?" The doctor seemed to be relaxing a bit.

Nat nodded.

"And is your voice always raspy like it is now?" he asked.

She shook her head from side to side.

"Well it looks like you are suffering from T.M.F." He had a twinkle in his eye.

"T-M-what?" I asked.

"Too Much Fun. She has irritated her vocal chords from screaming too much. Get a good night's sleep and don't talk a lot for the next couple of days." The doctor obviously enjoyed giving the prognosis.

It was a quiet drive back to the cottage. And every once and a while, when the moonlight found its way into the cockpit, I could make out a little grin on Natalie's face.

T.M.F. was already festering in its victim, Natalie, while she was being towed in a rubber tube.

16. E.D.'s Revenge

According to his many friends and business associates, my twin brother, Larry, is an all-round good guy. He enjoys life, is devoted to his wife and three children and runs a lucrative real estate brokerage business. Larry loves his small fleet of vehicles consisting of a BMW 540, a Chevy Silverado pick-up, a Volvo Cross Country, a Mustang Cobra convertible and a mint 1971 Datsun 240 Z sports car.

We never argue and he is always available. But Larry has an eccentric thirst for practical jokes, especially with family members. Although we are all aware of this, he has a surprising success rate when it comes to 'getting someone' with a 'good one'. April Fool's Day, a favorite for Larry, has seen him convince my parents to wait hours for him at a bogus airport

Mum checked the mail, opened the bill from Rollie's and started to shake.

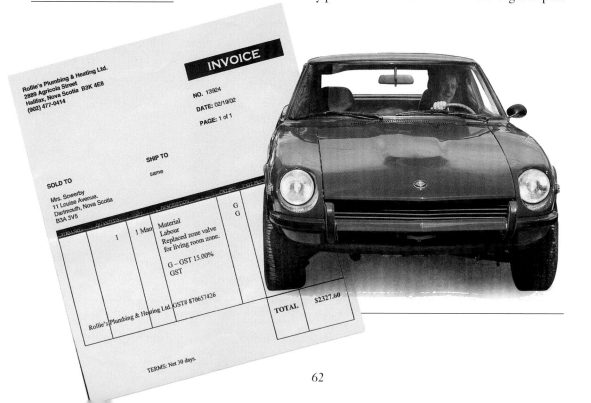

rendezvous and prepare special meals for no-show visits. He has gone miles out of his way to rattle chains in the wee hours around an old farm my parents bought and thought might be haunted.

My mother Edith, who we sometimes call E.D., recently had a problem with her furnace and called Larry whose business keeps him in touch with a variety of tradespeople.

"I'll sort it out," he told Mum, then called *Rollie's Plumbing and Heating* to check it out. *Rollie's* people were on the job within a couple of hours, quickly replacing a faulty zone valve. Delighted to have the situation resolved, E.D. promptly called to thank Larry.

Realizing an opportunity, Larry asked one of his employees to dummy-up a bill from *Rollie's Plumbing and Heating* and mail it to Mum so that it would arrive before the real invoice.

"Make it for $2,327.60." He chuckled, knowing the real charges wouldn't amount to much more than $100.

A couple of days later Mum checked the mail, opened the fake bill from *Rollie's* and started to shake. She felt nauseous. Remembering Larry was in Florida on holidays, she called my sister, Susan, and unloaded.

"They were only here twenty minutes. The part was the size of a telephone receiver for crying out loud!" She was riled up.

With limited expertise on heating systems, Susan tried to pacify her with talk about Mum's big house and the cost of technology. Not satisfied, Mum called *Rollie's Plumbing and Heating* to give them a piece of her mind.

"What are you trying to do, kill an old lady?" She immediately got to the point but soon smelled a rat as *Rollie's* politely explained that her bill for $151.65 had not even been mailed. Then it dawned on her… the chains at the farm, April Fool's day at the airport… LARRY!

A couple of days later while taking out the trash cans, struggling not to scratch Larry's 240 Z that had been parked in her garage all winter, she hatched a plan. Then, over the next few days, she presented it to Larry in a surprisingly believable way.

She had Susan tell him of a major motion picture being filmed near her home in Chester, Nova Scotia. It was to be a period piece set in the 1970s and the producers needed a 240 Z Datsun for one of the key scenes. Of course, Larry offered his beloved car. The 'film guy' called a few days later and explained they would need the car for one or two days for

A faulty zone valve in E.D.'s heating system set the stage for family shenanigans.

sequences to be shot with actor Peter Fonda.

There was plenty of excitement throughout the Sowerby clan leading up to the big day. While Mum's allies checked out the film location, made plans and avoided eye contact with Larry, he was busy detailing the Z and telling his wife and kids that, at $1,000 a day, the Datsun was finally going to put food on the table.

"They've certainly been eating a lot of crow," he gloated, explaining how he had been getting heat about hanging on to the temperamental old sports car for the past 12 years.

Larry told everyone he knew about the gig and even rented a trailer to carry the Z to the film location 50 kilometres east of Halifax at an abandoned fish plant. He would tow it in his matching red Chevy pick-up truck. Friends asked him to get autographs from Peter Fonda while my mother and sister suffocated in guilt over Larry's enthusiasm.

"It's been a hard week on my stomach," Susan told me a couple of days before the 'shoot'. Terrified of a face-to-face meeting with her son, Mum considered leaving town for the final days leading up to the Sting.

On the morning of the 'shoot', I helped Larry load the 240 Z onto the trailer. He was in an upbeat mood as he told me he'd hardly slept the night before and hadn't felt this excited since his last child was born. I had a hard time keeping a straight face driving to the 'shoot' location.

I had to bite my lip as Larry unloaded the Datsun at the abandoned fish plant.

"You know Garry, I'll remember this day for the rest of my life. Meeting Peter Fonda, the Datsun earning its keep." He was thrilled. "And even though I love that car, if they offered me $10,000 I'd let them blow it up!"

"Yes Larry, I'm sure you'll remember today for a long time," I offered as we turned into the driveway to the fish plant.

But there were no cars around the fish plant. No transport trucks. No lights or make-up trailers either. Larry looked confused as we walked around front to the wharf where a lone fisherman sat with his back to us toying with a fishing pole.

"The film shoot's not here obviously. Maybe that old geezer knows something about it," I suggested.

The scene had an *X Files* feeling. Larry tapped the fisherman on the shoulder then went slack-jawed as the 'geezer' turned around. I noticed a *Rollie's Plumbing and Heating* hat on his head.

"WWWhat is this?" Larry stuttered, staggering backwards while trying to process the vision of his mother looking up at him.

"*E.D.'s Revenge*," she whispered.

The joke was on Larry as the Sowerby family rallied to help E.D. extract revenge on her son.

17. *East Coast Redeye*

Lisa and I were psyched as we slid into the plush leather seats and fastened our seatbelts. We familiarized ourselves with the adjustment features while chatting about the overnight long haul we were buckling in for. After a barrage of meetings in Detroit and Toronto our Business Class surroundings were a welcome touch where we could relax, unwind and even catch a little sleep during the upcoming 18-hour voyage.

We were not about to lift off for Tasmania or Tierra del Fuego though. In fact, it was not a flight at all, although the amenities of our new GMC Yukon XL were right up there with any Business Class I've ever flown. The three rows of leather seats, killer sound system, power glass sunroof and OnStar system would keep us comfortable and entertained in the

high-end go-anywhere cruiser.

Our launch pad for the 1,700-kilometre drive to Halifax, Nova Scotia was a parking lot in downtown Toronto. It was 4:00 on Friday afternoon. The fuel was topped up, there were 40 music CDs in the centre console and our baggage was neatly packed behind the third row of seats. We didn't need a map. I'd driven the route dozens of times.

I discussed the virtues of the trip with Lisa, a novice at all-night road trips. I'd been on many over the years and wanted to see the first glow of morning on the road with Lisa right there beside me. Check her out at first light.

Escaping Toronto's gridlocked highways took an hour and a half.

The plan was to make Halifax by noon the next day in time to take our youngest daughter to her Saturday dance class.

Lisa horsed the storm-grey Yukon through downtown to the Don Valley Parkway where gridlocked commuters were escaping the workweek. It took an hour and a half to reach the outskirts of Toronto where we found a deserted parking lot and got into a bout of giddies while changing from business duds to road clothes.

Back on the highway, it was still bumper to bumper but things soon started to open up as the tailgaters and erratic lane changers peeled off exit by exit. Commuters, we suspected, wound tight from a day of wheeling and dealing and anxious to switch into home mode. On the other hand we figured the well-spaced cars executing crisp lane changes were probably out there for the long haul, accepting that for the time being life will consist of driving, thinking and getting into 'road groove'.

"What now?" Two hours later Lisa lays it on me. She had a 'let's eat' look on her face.

"A meal on the horizon is something to look forward to." I replied, feeling somewhat peckish. "Delay it as long as possible without getting cranky."

Over the next few hours, we listened to music while I read Lisa excerpts from the owners manual of our new Yukon. After a couple of hours, I was having trouble trying to figure out if the disgruntled look on Lisa's face was the result of slow starvation or if she was getting sick of hearing me try to calculate the distance a piston travelled for each revolution of the rear wheels.

We cleared Montreal just past midnight and slipped into the essence of the all-nighter.

Near the Quebec border, we pulled into Réal's Truck Stop. While I theorized a correlation between drive-thru dining and an increased rate of food ingestion, Lisa maneuvered through the parking lot crammed with idling transport trucks.

Inside, Réal's reminded me of a manufacturing plant's cafeteria as an eclectic assortment of truck drivers joked, ate and shuffled back and forth to the restrooms. Some quietly stared at their coffee looking a shade road-droned. But when they left, instead of going back to forklifts or assembly lines, they would be crawling into massive rigs and heading out into the night.

While a well-endowed waitress hovered, Lisa and I perused the menu, zeroing in on the chicken section. I ordered a half-chicken dinner and Lisa a hot chicken sandwich, which we correctly assumed, would have the same gravy. That seemed like a big thing to us as we soaked up the ambience of Réal's.

Back on the road I drove and settled into the rhythm of the traffic en route the Montreal decision. Once on Montreal Island, I normally take a right onto Decarie Boulevard and cross the Champlain Bridge for a quick look at the skyline. But I've always felt the tunnel across the Saint Lawrence River was faster. It's usually a last minute decision and since Lisa had fallen asleep, I went for the tunnel. We cleared Montreal just past midnight and slipped into the essence of the all-nighter.

After Lisa woke up, I explained some of the rules I've always followed.

"If it even crosses your mind that you need a break, take one. Keep egos at bay and forget you have only driven for a half-hour. Don't wait till your head snaps back and don't feel guilty about waking your partner. If you're both beat, then park for a while."

Music is a good way to get through those early morning hours. I like the ballads that give you something to think about. You can play instrument panel games making poker hands out of odometer readings. Cover the

odometer and clock and play guessing games with time and distance. Learning to estimate the distance to something you can see down the road comes in handy impressing your kids later.

But the best thing about an all-nighter is daybreak. Awaiting the big event, Lisa and I swapped turns in the 'chaise longue' we created by folding down the middle seats, strapping into the third row and stretching out.

Lisa was deep into the chaise when I pulled into the Tim Horton's Coffee Shop in Edmunston, New Brunswick. Men and women in orange hunting garb were quietly stocking up with thermoses of coffee and boxes of Timbits for the last day of deer hunting season.

As the sun cracked the horizon, we cranked up a country gospel CD I had found in a bargain bin at an Albuquerque truck stop.

We fueled an hour later in Plaster Rock, at the beginning of a 135-kilometre stretch of short-cut known as the Renous Woods. More fluorescent orange people through there mulling around waiting for daybreak which started as a faint glow on the twisty two-laner through the core of New Brunswick.

Daylight was a delight after the 14-hour November night. As the sun cracked the horizon, we cranked up a country gospel CD I had found in a bargain bin at an Albuquerque truck stop years earlier. *Walkin' in Jerusalem* deep in the Renous Woods.

The Saturday morning Farmer's Market in Moncton proved a rewarding pit stop. We looked like the living dead skulking around in search of cappuccino and sausage sandwiches.

Lisa drove most of the final leg to Halifax. As I drifted in and out of consciousness, I thought about how cheerful and eager she had been at first light back in the Renous woods. We pulled into our driveway 18 hours and 10 minutes after leaving Toronto.

"Do you still love me?" My breath reminded me of the smell of an electric train set I had as a kid.

"Ask me after my shower," she laughed.

18. No Showers for the Fly

"What happened to my pyramid of brownies?" Lisa clucked from the kitchen. For a Sunday morning, her tone was surprisingly brisk.

I confessed to an early morning case of the munchies that resulted in minor samplings. I told her the incident also involved two home-made dips she had slaved over the night before. Then I gently softened her by waxing on about a correlation between her cooking ability and the incident. Obviously, if she wasn't such a good cook, the raid would never have happened.

In the wee morning hours, the inside of the fridge had looked like a

well-stocked Montreal delicatessen. Not surprising, after the cache of wine Lisa dragged home the day before along with bags of mysterious ingredients for patés, desserts and other yummy stuff I was not supposed to touch. The kitchen became a 'Garry no-go zone' while the phone rang off the wall with calls about the bridal shower Lisa was throwing for our future sister-in-law, Erin Baird.

"Alright. I can rebuild the brownie pyramid and smooth over the fork marks in the dip, but you still have to make yourself scarce today." Lisa had that I'm-Martha-Stewart-and-I-can-do-anything look.

I was banned from my own home so a gaggle of Erin's friends and relatives could partake in the hazy world of a female-only bridal shower. Hazy, because I've never been able to get a clear explanation as to what goes on at a bridal shower other than vague descriptions of shower games and crustless sandwiches.

This spider and the Fly kept me company during my exile.

I decided the six hours of limbo would be an opportunity to drive one of my cars that had not had a run for a while. So I fished into the key box and pulled out the key to our 1991 4-door Pontiac Firefly.

It's silver with no tape deck, cruise control or power options. Without even a rear wiper, the base unit of the 1991 General Motors line-up is absolutely bottom-of-the-line. Just a radio with four tinny speakers. A spider my daughter Natalie made from a piece of egg carton 8 years ago dangles from the rearview mirror.

I leased it as an office run-around car 11 years ago. At the time, its three-cylinder motor was one of the stingiest fuel users on the market. I rationalized its existence by theorizing the fuel savings over my eclectic fleet of guzzlers would cover the payments. When the lease was up, I purchased what has turned out to be an exceptionally trouble-free vehicle. With its perfect finish, the rust-free little econo-box looks like it just came out of the carton.

We all call it the Fly. And I will keep it forever, because no one else would!

Just before leaving, Lisa asked if I wanted a sandwich for the road. My stomach flipped considering the nasal delights permeating the house. She handed me a plate of crusts from the trimmed shower sandwiches. Minute scraps of filling clung to a few of them.

The cell phone rang before I got out of the driveway. It was Mum

The 1991 Firefly is the absolute bottom of the line, not even a rear wiper.

hinting for a drive downtown with her friend Catherine. I told her about my exile and thanked her for giving me something to do.

"What are you driving?" She quizzed, obviously hoping for something exotic.

"The Fly." After 11 years she knew what I meant.

"We'll take the bus then," she laughed, then agreed to my services.

I snapped photographs of them getting out of the car in front of a throng of Sunday strollers along side a downtown park. Mum and Catherine were all dolled up for an afternoon concert and I made the most of the opportunity.

"Everybody must think we're big shots," Mum whispered as I said goodbye.

"Yeah," I said pointing to the diminutive silver sub-compact. "Real shakers in this big Firefly."

I couldn't help slinking around my neighborhood after leaving them. I went by our house hoping for a glimpse of bridal shower action. On the way, I saw an old friend and pulled over to chat. I could tell from his body language that he didn't get my rationale for hanging on to a 1991 Firefly when I had a garage full of capable cars and trucks.

I drove around aimlessly all afternoon. The putter of the tiny 3-cylinder engine and the whine of its 5-speed manual transmission kept me amused for a while. I listened to an 'oldies' AM radio station and reminisced about the two-week business trip I had taken in the Fly to Nashville, Tennessee.

I had rendezvous-ed with my brother Larry on the side of the Trans-Canada somewhere in New Brunswick. Ensconced in the Fly, I was surrounded by a laptop computer, two cell phones, three cameras and a case of files.

Larry looked down from his Chevy Suburban as I rambled about programs I was working on: consulting with people in England about a proposed around-the-world car race; a sale for a movie we were producing was imminent and I had to be ready to fly to Los Angeles at a moment's notice... So much to do, so little Fly space to work in. Larry pegged me as a manic depressive cruising around in his Firefly swamped with delusions of power and grandeur.

The reminiscing was fine but after a few hours I got Flyed out. However, since it was my duty to keep away from house and family until 6:00 pm, I carried on. Shortly after six, Lisa called, ending my exile. I parked in the driveway and exchanged pleasantries with hangers-on in the backyard. Inside, while greeting the exuberant bride-to-be, I surveyed the scene for evidence of bridal shower game activity.

The dining room looked like the aftermath of a Roman feast. And there, among the dregs of gourmand delights, I spotted the remains of my old friend, the brownie pyramid.

There were a few left so I popped one into my mouth. But I left the rest on the plate, in case I woke up in the middle of the night with another case of the munchies.

Lisa (right) celebrates with her future sister-in-law Erin Baird.

19. *Vibe-Rating Roadies Go The Distance*

I figured morning at the stunning Num-Ti-Jah Lodge overlooking Alberta's Bow Lake Glacier would be different. So I lay wide-awake for a few long minutes before sneaking a look at the digital alarm clock beside my 15th bed in as many days.

In the silence, I tried to convince myself that this time the clock wouldn't register the ungodly hour of 4:11 a.m. that was getting so familiar. But thoughts of the day ahead soon revved me up, my eyes popped open and there it was: a four and an eleven staring me in the face.

Yes, the ever-present 'Drive the Vibe' was reminding me more and more of the movie *Amityville Horror* where the primary characters wake up at the exact same time every day. But the similarity always ended when

Roadies (left to right) Bill Rumsey, Lisa Calvi, Peter Schlay and Heather Capstick display stress cracks.

my bare feet hit the floors of a mishmash of unlikely accommodations between Halifax, Nova Scotia and Vancouver, British Columbia.

A few months earlier, the folks at General Motors had asked us for a bid to develop a cross-Canada media event. The General was launching a new car called the Pontiac Vibe and, considering our notorious Canadian winter climate, reckoned a cross-country drive would avoid the possibility of a brutal snowstorm blowing out an event staged in a single location.

Our job would be to develop and referee an engaging road game for up to 60 competing journalists armed with a technological concoction of laptop computers, cellular phones, RIM Blackberry devices and digital cameras. Results would be played out to a virtual internet audience as the trans-continental quest unfolded.

In the weeks leading up to the mid-February start date, GM recruited three relay teams of 20 journalists each. Meanwhile Lisa and I drove more than half an equator length back and forth across Canada building the framework of the 9,000-kilometre road game.

Our intent was to produce an event that would show the journalists and Canadians just what the Great White North has to offer during the worst possible time for a cross-Canada driving trek.

In late February, Lisa, myself and a three-person support team

Top: Journalists Paul Fleet and Howard Elmer
Middle: A big axe to grind in Nackawic, New Brunswick
Bottom: Roadside Indian head mural in Quebec
Bottom left: Departing Num-Ti-Jah Lodge in Bow Lake, Alberta

The Ice Hotel near Quebec City on the shores of Lac St-Joseph. A unique winter attraction that vanishes every spring.

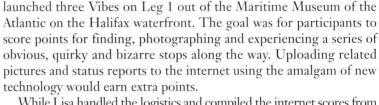

launched three Vibes on Leg 1 out of the Maritime Museum of the Atlantic on the Halifax waterfront. The goal was for participants to score points for finding, photographing and experiencing a series of obvious, quirky and bizarre stops along the way. Uploading related pictures and status reports to the internet using the amalgam of new technology would earn extra points.

While Lisa handled the logistics and compiled the internet scores from our Halifax office, our roadies, Newfoundlander Bill Rumsey, volunteer fireman-cum-real-estate-agent Peter Schlay and Nova Scotia Museum marketing officer Heather Capstick helped keep the wheels of the non-stop brain cramp in motion.

Along the way we solved plenty of behind-the-scenes problems. We rescheduled rooms in Rocanville, Saskatchewan after getting bumped by a chinchilla convention, arbitrated the team relay points and visited plenty of small-town car washes. We convinced the City of Moncton to plow the snow off Magnetic Hill for the first time, sent teams ice fishing on snowmobiles and endured midnight fire alarms.

Our guests feasted on moose meat in an isolated fishing camp and relaxed at Sunday dinner with all the trimmings at a prairie farmhouse. One freezing night, a whole town turned out and threw a curling party for the journalists.

The interiors of our support vehicles looked like mobile command posts. While inverters to run computers hummed, walkie-talkies crackled and cell phones chirped, Heather and I raced ahead setting up the 34 overnight and lunch venues. Meanwhile Bill and Pete swept the routes looking for problems to sort out. At night we became Vibe-raters, scoring the daily results. We juggled more than 200 activity options. We chased gremlins around the technology.

When we reached Vancouver, we went our separate ways. I got back to dealing with Lisa in a non-virtual way. Bill Rumsey rallied the wrenches in his service bay at Hickman Motors in St. John's and Peter Schlay strapped on his real estate job in Halifax. Heather Capstick probably reached for her seatbelt more than once sitting at her desk in the Nova Scotia Museum.

The trusty Vibes became just another list of stock numbers and the journalists turned their attentions elsewhere. Hopefully, the marketing and public relations people at General Motors patted themselves on the back for the novel, engaging way the event helped Canadians look at themselves, their country and the new Vibe.

The Odyssey roadies were happy for a successful conclusion but sad to see the end of the unrelenting 'Drive the Vibe' program. And I was relieved to wake up to a clock that didn't read 4:11 a.m.

Top: A Northwest Mounted Police you wouldn't want to mess with in Redvers, Saskatchewan

Bottom: Winnie the Pooh's home in White River, Ontario

77

20. Please, No Rough Idling!

I was half expecting Audrey Yates' call since she had leased a Volkswagen Golf the same month Lisa leased her VR6-GTI. Lisa was buying out her lease and I knew Audrey, a savvy marketing consultant, would want my opinion on what to do.

Calls like hers come a few times a year. Sometimes it's an old friend like Audrey, though it could be a close relative or even an obscure acquaintance. They chat me up about family and what's going on at work, often offering tasty tidbits of gossip before getting to their automotive needs.

Audrey's Golf had low mileage. She is a single, career woman so the interior had not been trashed by a brood of rambunctious kids or a rowdy rottweiler. The exterior had a few minor blemishes, the kind to be expected

with someone who isn't a 'car nerd' like myself. She could have bought out her lease since, with only 52,000 kilometres, the Golf would provide many more years of reliable motoring.

I figured she had two other options. Getting a new car would be a clean start along with the excitement that comes with a fresh set of wheels. Finding a winter clunker and revisiting the situation in the spring had merit, too. I'd have gone for the clunker and savored the big decision until spring which would have resulted in two car-fever hits. But I knew Audrey would want to do the 'right' thing for her 'situation'.

As I found myself being pulled into her predicament, I thought back to the early 1960s when my grandfather wanted to trade his pink 1959 Vauxhall Velox for a new car. A stroke had left him with a partially paralyzed right hand that rendered the Vauxhall's column-mounted three-speed manual shifter problematic. Grampy was finally going to buy a car with an automatic transmission.

At the time, my father was driving a 1963 Mercury Custom Monterey. The peacock turquoise, 300-horsepower unit with a 'breezeway' rear window was road candy to my older brother Bruce, who had just gotten his driver's license. Dad located an identically coloured '63 Comet at the Mercury dealer and suggested Gramps buy that. My grandfather liked it, so Dad spent a week hammering out a deal for the Comet.

My grandparents, Robert and Rita Sowerby with their rough-idling '63 Mercury Comet.

The Comet's 'Big 6' powerplant had adequate performance but it never idled as smoothly as the Vauxhall's engine. If Grampy placed a glass of water on the hood, there was too much surface turbulence for his liking. And so began a parade of visits to the Mercury dealership to rectify the rough idle.

"Poor car. Poorest car I ever had!" It drove Dad nuts.

Every time he saw my grandfather, those words found their way into the conversation. Grampy had gone deaf when he was 14 but even as a senior, he still remembered how to speak very clearly. His volume, however, was about twice what was required in most situations. When he was excited it got even louder, borderline yelling. Sometimes I'd be up in my bedroom drifting off to sleep and I'd hear it through the floorboards.

"Poor car. Poorest car I ever had!" I knew my Grandparents were visiting.

So the peacock turquoise Mercury Comet resulted in one of the most

Audrey Yates is thrilled with her new Volkswagen Jetta and claims she will keep it forever.

direct pieces of advice my father ever gave me. Don't advise someone on what car to buy, which was precisely where I was headed with Audrey.

Within a few days, Audrey and I were at the local VW dealer. Rows of shiny Golfs, Jettas and Passats glistened in the bright winter sunlight. I suggested she maintain the status quo and move into a new Golf. Upgrade to power windows and cruise control. A sun roof perhaps, to make her feel sporty on those summer beach days.

"Why would I get another Golf? They look pretty much the same as my old one. And the Jetta sedans resemble everything else out there on the market." I detected an edge of panic in her voice, but my father's advice kept me in check.

Then her face changed. The stress disappeared. She beamed. Her voice became girlish as she gazed across the lot, honing in on a new blue Jetta station wagon. I had never seen one before and immediately liked it.

"I could put so much in it. My gardening supplies. It's so cute!" She was hooked.

Audrey asked if I would negotiate the deal for her. Just let her go home and wait for me to convince the dealer to go for her price. The last thing I remembered before agreeing was my grandfather's booming mantra about the Comet's rough idle.

The negotiations lasted six weeks. To make Audrey's desired numbers work, she had to find a buyer for her Golf. Dad's advice haunted me every time she called with an update.

"How does this sound for the newspaper ad? Tell me again how the tax works? What if I sell it out of province? What about the rust spot on the grill? Am I doing the right thing?"

In the end it all worked out. Audrey sold her Golf at the price she wanted and the VW dealer patiently held on to her Jetta wagon with a minimal deposit. She's thrilled with her new car and claims she will keep it forever.

Tonight Audrey is coming over for dinner. We'll talk business for a while, scheme about Caribbean holidays that will never happen and talk about old times. She and Lisa may even gang up on me for being insensitive about something, and that will be fine.

As long as I don't hear anything about a rough idle.

21. *Reduce, Reuse, Recycle*

When I pulled up to the house at the end of a four-day business trip, a Honda Civic Hybrid was sitting in my driveway. Lisa had picked it up the day before and we were going to use it for a trip to a quasi-communal farmhouse in which friends Jon Clark and Karen Ramsland have been involved since the early 1970s, before the onset of responsibility and careers. It would be a chance for us to get a weekend in the countryside while checking out the Hybrid's miserly road manners.

Top: Lisa felt no guilt doubling up after our fuel-stingy weekend.

Bottom: Colin Harmer had better luck planking salmon than flying his remote-controlled model airplane.

Alternate-powered vehicles are no strangers to me. I own two diesel GMC trucks and a propane-powered Checker taxi cab that I bought in 1982 to enter a race that never happened. I ran a series of disappointing performance tests on a rudimentary electric car for the military in the mid '70s. But since then, other than bouts with bumper cars at the odd amusement park, I've had limited contact with electric, or hybrid gas-electric, vehicles.

Lisa gave me the lowdown on the Civic Hybrid's propulsion system. Its small 4-cylinder engine has an electric motor positioned in front of its transmission. The electric motor provides assistance when climbing hills or accelerating. During braking or deceleration, the system captures energy in a storage battery for use on the next hill climb or speed change. There's nothing to plug in, nothing to recharge.

I approached what looked like a normal Honda Civic with skeptical curiosity.

While driving, the instrumentation displays whether you are being assisted by the electric motor or capturing kinetic energy usually lost as heat during conventional braking. Every time I hit the brakes or coasted down a hill, I felt like I was getting a prize. The system was giving me something back to use later.

As a nifty bonus, the gasoline engine automatically shuts off at stops rendering a silence that made me feel somewhat self-righteous at busy crosswalks.

I explained the features to my 16-year-old daughter, who has taken a much keener interest in cars since she got her beginner driver's licence.

"This is it. This is the future, right here, Dad!" Her eyes were almost popping out of her head.

The more I drove it, the more determined I became to squeeze the absolute most out of each litre of fuel. I figured my emerging 'green' feelings would be a good conversation piece over the weekend at the farmhouse where common sense consumption has been a mantra for years.

On the way to The Farm, Lisa drove and her friend Rhonda sat up front so they could catch up on the latest gossip. I sat in the back reading a book called *Extreme Encounters*. Every now and then I would read them excerpts about what it felt like to be buried alive, mauled by a grizzly bear or executed in an electric chair. They tended to ignore me except when Lisa wanted to dispose of an apple core, handing it to me with a take-care-of-this look.

At The Farm, energy conservation was underway big-time. Rhonda's husband, Colin Harmer, was not having any luck starting a new remote-controlled airplane's engine. Jon couldn't get his remote-controlled car going either. I felt proud that we were all doing our bit for the environment.

Jon and Karen were gracious hosts. They showed us around the gardens and walking trails. They had a thriving compost area and their recycling bins were lined up and clearly labeled. There were two Volvo station wagons in the yard.

They prepared a scrumptious meal of planked salmon, fresh corn and yummy Greek salad. After dinner, we looked at old photos of the farmhouse under varying degrees of renovation during its metamorphosis from a rundown dwelling into a laid-back weekend escape from the city grind.

The evening had provided the kind of relaxation I had been looking for. Sleep came easily in one of the upstairs bunkbeds.

Above: Jon Clark and Greg Smiley (right) got into the dirty work.

Below: The Farm at Wallace Bay, Nova Scotia.

Reduce, Reuse, Recycle

Top: Jon and Karen's dog, Lily, takes a breather.

Bottom: Getting the most out of the Honda Civic Hybrid's miserly ways became the name of the game at The Farm.

In the morning, I volunteered to help out on a water conservation project they had been trying to sort out for months. Jon and his business partner and co-owner of the house, Greg Smiley, had misaligned 'the hole' and 'the seat' of an outhouse they were repositioning. I did calculations and provided advice while they notched out new floorboards and jimmied the outhouse enough to align the critical components. After a few hours of tee hees and some all-too-predictable toilet humour, the project was successfully completed.

Everyone was impressed with our diligence in carrying out the task. The old farmhouse's indoor plumbing would get a break during peak toiletry periods and guests would have the option to enjoy a good old-fashioned outdoor experience.

After lunch we bid farewell. Colin's remote-controlled airplane was still on the blink and all the outhouse needed was a fresh coat of interior paint. Down the road, I checked the Hybrid's 'assist – charge' gauge. It was in the neutral zone, nothing gained, nothing lost.

But there was a downhill stretch ahead and that gauge would soon remind me that driving a Civic Hybrid was a much more civilized way to conserve resources than moving an antique outhouse.

22. The Funky Museum Roadshow

"The only time I tried to ride one of these I went over the handle bars and bruised my ribs so badly they hurt for a year." Peter Duffy, a columnist for Halifax's Chronicle Herald newspaper, was dead serious.

When my instructor, a blacksmith who looked like he was chiselled from granite, told me it took him a day to get the hang of it, panic raced through my veins. After all, I had only seen a Penny-Farthing bicycle once before and the idea of piloting one around in front of a handful of tourists was not high on my list of things to do.

Layla Calvi reports her '20' before movin' on.

I climbed up and shoved off. It was shaky but the wobbles soon disappeared. I zipped past the crowd and down the streets of Sherbrooke Village, a restored 19th-century Nova Scotian town, feeling like a 4-year-old who had ripped off his training wheels and blasted off on a Tour de France. And as I rode the streets dressed in a farmer's period costume, I was frozen in time.

During a zany 9-day visit to 43 eclectic museums and heritage sites of Nova Scotia, I found myself in many new situations. As Lisa and Heather Capstick from the Nova Scotia Museum followed in a support car, Peter and I wound a 3500-kilometre route around the province in my old blue and white Volvo. Our quest? To find the 25 funkiest things in the Nova Scotia Museum system.

Sure Red Cloud, the 245DL station wagon my old college buddy Ken Langley and I drove around the world in 1980, was a star. Almost half a million kilometres on the clock and we never opened the toolbox, not once. But the real stars were the Nova Scotians along the way. Not just the public, but the folks at the hotels and restaurants that provided meals and accommodations. And those who opened up their museums and their imaginations and showed us their funk.

Plenty of firsts. I kept rhythm in a band with a master drummer from Ghana. We sheared sheep. Twenty-six grade 4 school children tied a rope to Red Cloud's roo-bar and towed us through the streets of Yarmouth singing renditions of 18th-century sea shanties dedicated to that old Volvo's exploits. I learned how to make rappie pie and pulled a lobster trap from the bottom of the sea floor. I did time with Peter in a 19th century jailhouse.

Driving? How about a yoked team of oxen. I learned to drive a buckboard, just like Ben Cartwright did on *Bonanza*. Two big horsepower. I piloted a one-lunged sailboat, the *Maud RM*, across Lunenburg Harbour, and did a stint behind the wheel of a 1931 Model A Ford. Peter and I lost big time in the Mount Temple potato race.

The judging was the hard part. An art contest, a colouring contest, a decorated bike contest, and even a 1940s attire contest. I picked out the best replica of Red Cloud made of recycled materials and judged a funky chicken contest. I can't believe how hard that was. I've never judged anything before. And having to choose just one winner when twenty-five

7-year-olds are staring at you with 'pick mine' written on their faces left me feeling like a heel.

Meanwhile, Lisa was filling the Funk Log and the more I judged, the more I realized how hard it would be to pick winners. By the time we hit the finish line, the log contained 125 funk contenders which had to be cut to 25, one in five. How do you give up a curved closet door with a hole cut in it for cats to chase mice through or a mirrored ball hanging in a window to ward off witches. And what about Gus, the 77-year-old turtle, who crawled away and came back two weeks later?

How about a prototype of a portable female urinal circa 1901, patent still pending? Or the Sturgeon sex quiz? Or the anti-lick device on the dog-powered butter churner or out-flinging Peter in the sheep dung-flinging contest? We heard the story about the ship's captain that lost the bell of his Lunenburg-based fishing trawler in rough seas off the Grand Banks of Newfoundland. Eighteen years later, fishing in the same area, his son pulls the corroded bell up in a fishing net. Funky.

But my favorite funk story was the fate of the Cumberland Queen, a Nova Scotian-built ocean freighter loaded with salt that sank off

Heather Capstick welcomes the Roadshow to the Museum of Natural History in Halifax, Nova Scotia

Partner in Funk, Peter Duffy, took time from his duty as the diligent scribe (above) to pinch-hit for a 'squeegie kid' on Red Cloud's windshield.

Cape Hatteras in 1922. The next year locals were stunned to wake up one morning and find she had risen to the surface and, after a clean-up, the Cumberland Queen plied the seven seas for another 30 years. Very funky.

We crossed the finish line with grins on our faces and an eel pot full of lupins on the roof. The children and folks of Stellarton welcomed us back to our start point at the Museum of Industry with wild cheers and a funky band. More cheers as we wheeled that old Volvo into its feature display room beside the two GMC Trucks in which we set our south-north records so long ago.

We had been treated like visiting relatives time and time again. Peter and I had become road cronies. Later that night, in Halifax, I sat on my back porch with the Funk Log and its 125 entries. I read and laughed. And thought. And laughed. And then I did one of the most difficult things I have ever done.

I whittled the Funk Log down to the top 25. And even though they all couldn't be there, what we encountered reinforced my belief that with its people, geography and heritage, Nova Scotia is a darn funky place.

The Funk

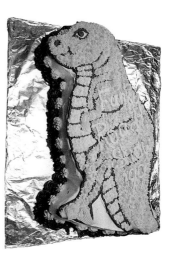

1. **Lobster - The King of Funk** - anything that can travel 25 feet per second in reverse, has invisible blood and comes in blue, white, orange and red is funky. Add to that the fact that it can throw a claw if being attacked - and grow one back in a year elevates the lobster to King of Funk. *Fisheries Museum of the Atlantic, Lunenburg*

2. **Einstein the Funky Chicken** - a chicken with attitude, style and plenty of funk. One look says it all. *Ross Farm Museum, New Ross*

3. **Red Cloud is Blue and White - Bias Funk** - why would a blue and white car be named Red Cloud? *Museum of Industry, Stellarton*

4. **Jerry Burke's Running Shoes** - walked 340 kilometres from Halifax to Arichat, for a woman they say... *LeNoir Forge Museum, Arichat*

5. **Rosebank Cottage** - 182-year old cottage built by soldiers, not one straight board in the place. *Ross Farm Museum, New Ross*

6. **Hank Snow - Country Funk** - started out as a cabin boy on a Liverpool Schooner and evolved to one of the biggest names in the history of country music. *Hank Snow Country Music Centre, Liverpool*

7. **"Pop" Bottle** - discover why soda is called pop. *Musee Acadien, Pubnico-Ouest*

8. **Green Highlander in a Brandy Snifter** - made of moose mane and African bird feathers. *Margaree Salmon Museum, North East Margaree*

9. **Funky Pickles** - jar of pickles brought to the surface from the wreck of the Cedar Grove that went down near Canso in 1882. *Whitman House Museum, Canso*

A million kernels of corn on the wall, a million kernels of corn, take one down...

10. **Eel Pot** - will hold up to 200 eels. The ones that don't end up in an eel pot will migrate to England, taking two years to get there. *Fisherman's Life Mseum, Jeddore Oyster Pond*

11. **Mom Suze** - born 10 March 1883 in Cherry Brook, raised 19 children and lived to the age of 105 years. *Black Cultural Centre, Dartmouth*

12. **Cod Skin Bikini** - say no more. *Fisheries Museum of the Atlantic, Lunenburg*

13. **Periwinkle Table - Double Funk** - funky-looking and must have smelled funky somewhere along the line as it dried out. *Musee Acadien, Pubnico-Ouest*

14. **Haggis - Mysterious Funk** - haggis and kids don't mix, can't make original version because food laws won't allow the parts required. *Antigonish Heritage Museum, Antigonish*

15. **Halibut** - starts out as an up and down fish then turns on its side; its eyeball migrates up to the top so it can lay on the bottom and wait for food to swim by. *Fisheries Museum of the Atlantic, Lunenburg*

16. **Black House - 'Taieh Dubh'** - funky from its seaweed insulation to its indoor livestock pen. *Highland Village Museum, Iona*

17. **Double Hat - Bad Funk** - two hats, one worn close to the head to stop lice from jumping into your 'good' hat. *Cape Breton Centre for Heritage and Science*

18. **Wasp Bag - Tricky Funk** - stuffed paper bag hanging in a doorway to keep wasps, bees and hornets out of the house. *Jost House, Sydney*

19. **Amoskeag Steamer** - oldest surviving horse-drawn steamer in Canada, built in 1863. *Firefighters Museum of Nova Scotia, Yarmouth*

20. **The Sutherland Steam Mill - Funky Contraption -**
    The Sutherland Steam Mill, Denmark

21. **Hydroliquefication** - the process which turns coal into gas.
    Glace Bay Miners Museum, Glace Bay

22. **Breadbag Square Dancing Dress** - made by Louise Martinelli, a
    blind lady, out of Butternut breadbags.
    Yarmouth County Museum, Yarmouth

23. **Unknown Artifact** - an art deco-looking appliance that no one has
    been able to identify. *Yarmouth County Museum, Yarmouth*

24. **The 4-Holer** - a four-holer outhouse with a covered walkway leading
    from the main house. *Lawrence House Museum, Maitland*

25. **Funky Nova Scotians - The Evolution of Funk** - two to three
    hundred years ago, Nova Scotians bathed once a year if at all which
    was definitely low-end funk. Now we are flooded with good funk
    galore!

Centre photo: *Natalie Sowerby (right) and Susan Gillis get funky.*

Wanted: Single Male looking for voluptuous Yankee woman to support and marry. Must be a good farmer and have good ship building skills. Deck hands need not apply.

Funky MUSEUM ROADSHOW

There's **neat stuff** at Nova Scotia's museums!

23. Alone on a Family Vacation

When the idea surfaced for a 5-day, 2,500-kilometre road trip to visit my father-in-law, Paul Calvi and his wife Annie, on his 60th birthday, I got pretty excited. The drive from Halifax to Fitch Bay in Quebec's Eastern Townships would give Lisa and I a chance to unwind, relax and to entertain our two youngest daughters, twelve-year-old Layla and Natalie, 15. Between en route attractions, I would regale them with stories of road trips with my parents when I was their age in the 1960s. It would be an opportunity for learning and fellowship.

But selling them on a trip starting the first day of summer vacation was not easy. It meant goodbye to celebratory sleepovers, beach parties and getting together with the gang at someone's house to ponder the

Oblivious to their surroundings, Layla (left) and Natalie may as well have been back home in the den, but they sure were having fun.

forthcoming endless weeks of summer vacation. Getting stuffed into our GMC Yukon XL and hitting the road to visit their grandparents along with a gaggle of relatives they hardly knew was obviously inhumane treatment.

I sweetened the pitch with a string of enticements. Visits were planned to every amusement park en route including rides on *Le Monstre*, the awesome wooden rollercoaster at Montreal's La Ronde amusement park. I threw in stops at go-kart tracks we might encounter along the way.

Onboard entertainment? I had an inverter that would boost one of the Yukon's power outlets from 12 volts to the 110 volts needed to run a 15-inch television / VCR combo. They could indulge in those birthday videos they knew line-by-line or commandeer the truck's CD player at will. Washroom and munchie breaks were on demand. I'd be their slave, the minion behind the wheel bending to their every whim.

Prior to leaving, Lisa packed board games, magazines, snacks and travel books. I folded the center row of seats and secured the TV / VCR combo behind the driver's seat. At the last minute, Natalie and Layla ran for the PlayStation system then strapped themselves into the third row of seats and stretched out, limousine-style.

For the next ten hours, with the exception of a stop at an amusement park and a meal where Natalie bought a video of *America's Dumbest Criminals*, I motored on in silence while the girls belted out the words of every song in *The Sound of Music*. Lisa had crawled into the back and they had me crank up the air conditioner while they snuggled under a quilt. Up front, I froze as I tried to imagine the scenes back there on the tube with the tinny speaker from the TV blasting in my ears.

My mind flashed to road trips as a kid when the annual 1,000-kilometre run from Moncton to Montreal was right up there with Christmas in my books. Sleep was scarce the night before we'd cram ourselves into the family sedan for the two-day drive.

The trek, mostly on two-lane roads, usually featured a flat tire or two. Sometimes a water or fuel pump would go on one of the new Buick Specials or Mercury Montereys.

Dad drove. My mother, E.D., would hand around potato salad and roast beef or egg salad sandwiches from the onboard cooler. We had to keep the windows up most of the time because E.D. would have had a

The power inverter created a power struggle between the driver and the rear-seat passengers.

fresh hairdo for family festivities in Montreal. There was no parental bribery. Our idea of an attraction was to drive by a river dam or for Dad to snap the Buick into passing gear to get by someone on the twisty, pot-holed route through New Brunswick.

We'd make it past Rivière-du-Loup on the south shore of the Saint Lawrence on the first day. Dad would ask a local farmer if we could pitch the ugliest, hardest-to-put-up tent I've ever dealt with. We'd wrestle that smelly canvas into a home while E.D. would do dinner magic with the two-burner Coleman stove.

Sometimes Dad would run an all-nighter. Brothers Bruce and Larry and I would take shifts up front with him - just gazing over the reflection of street lights slipping by on the shiny metal dash as that tank of a car beat its way through the night. We kept Dad awake motor-mouthing about the engine, transmission and options on every Mercury Turn Pike Cruiser, Chevy Bel Air and Custom Royal Dodge we spotted.

But now we were cruise-controlled on a new four-lane along the rolling banks of the Saint John River, the girls vegged in the rear seat of the Yukon yodel-ay-ee-hoo-ing it with all eyes glued to Julie Andrews on the TV screen. Oblivious to their surroundings, they may as well have been back home in the den, but they sure were having fun.

By 11:00 that night, I was beat. Ignoring cries of foul about *Harry Potter and the Philosopher's Stone* not being finished, I forced an end to the techno-barrage by pulling into a spider-infested lodge for the night.

The next morning's drive was much of the same, only different voices from the TV. When *America's Dumbest Criminals* finished, and I was through trying to figure out what the bad guys looked like, everyone fell asleep and I was alone with only the hum of the inverter to entertain me.

E.D.'s creations on the Coleman stove kept brothers Bruce (left), Larry (centre) and I well-fed on the road.

Upon arrival at Paul and Annie's place, the girls raved about the great trip it was. After all, they had watched movies, played PlayStation or slept the entire way. But now they were anxious to get into the new pool that had just been installed.

I thought about the times so long ago, helping Dad fold the tent, creeped out by the daddy-long-leg spiders that seemed addicted to the dewy canvas.

"Oh well, they had a good time. Maybe the trip back will be different." I thought, eyeing the fuse on the inverter.

Lisa, Natalie and Layla pack up and head out for another day of the mobile film festival.

Chapter 4 It's More Impressive Actually Here Than When You See It On TV

By daybreak, I thought I was losing consciousness. It seemed ironic that after everything I'd been through, I was finally going to be brought down by a newsletter mailing.

24. *Wild Night at the Wild Rose*

I don't make a habit of staying in bed-and-breakfast accommodations. After a day of driving or business meetings, sitting around a parlor watching television with fellow residents isn't high on my priority list. Having breakfast with someone who wants to know what kind of dogs I have owned is not necessarily the kick-start I need in the morning either.

I don't want to feel guilty about messing up my room and sometimes I just want to lie on the bed and flick through the TV channels looking for *America's Most Wanted* without wondering who is shuffling down the hallway outside my bedroom door. I want to come and go anonymously.

On a trip to Texas I needed a place to hole up for a week while I checked out roads and amenities for an event we were developing. Glen Rose, a

"We're full, but try the Wild Rose Inn down the street," a polite, elderly gentleman with a lanky Texan drawl advised.

Sheilah Carter Keeling's southern charm helped change my perception of B&Bs.

small town 100 miles southwest of Dallas, seemed a logical place. I found a quaint inn not far from the looming courthouse on the central square and inquired about a room.

"We're full, but try the Wild Rose Inn down the street," a polite, elderly gentleman with a lanky Texan drawl advised.

The name conjured up images of untamed gardens and breezy verandahs so I dropped by the Wild Rose Inn. When I realized it was actually a bed-and-breakfast, my inclination was to bolt. But a cleaning lady spotted me and brought me into the house and introduced me to the owner, Sheilah Carter Keeling.

It didn't take long for Sheilah's charm and southern hospitality to unhinge my resistance to spending a week in a B&B.

"I set it up so y'all can go 'bout your business without botherin' me or me botherin' you," she explained with an impish grin.

Sheilah proudly escorted me through five delightfully different guest-rooms. Each had a private entrance so guests could come and go as they pleased from the rambling stucco house.

I settled on the Red Rose, a suite that had once been the garage, and pulled up out front. I felt like I was home, even my own driveway.

The suite consisted of a small, pleasantly furnished living room with a television and VCR. The rose-coloured bedroom was appointed with exquisite antiques including a mahogany four poster bed and frilly lampshades. The cavernous, marble-accented bathroom featured a party-sized whirlpool bath. Dainty doilies, tasteful draperies, feather pillows and a goose-down duvet all helped crumble my redneck attitude about B&Bs.

Over the next week, I checked out every back road and culvert in six counties around Glen Rose. At night I'd pull into the driveway, retreat into the comfy Red Rose suite and 'veg' in front of the television.

I looked forward to breakfast in Sheilah's eclectic dining room where her staff, Marilyn and Jennifer, fussed over me like a new pet. Sheilah showered me with stories about her past, her family and day-to-day life in slow-movin' Glen Rose.

I heard about possums breaking into her kitchen and the insurance settlement over her daughter's recent car accident. Her openness and enthusiasm continuously cheered me up.

Sheilah made me laugh a lot. She made my eyes water, too. And she made me want to make my bed in the morning and to not throw towels on the floor after my shower. Sheilah taught me that a 'double-take-down anything' was really good and said I could call her anything but a 'broad'.

One night, I decided to watch television from the bedroom section of my suite, à la Holiday Inn. With shaky legs, I lugged an early model 'portable' television set from the living room and placed it in a precarious position on top of the dainty antique dresser near the foot of the bed. I hooked up the VCR and put on *Monster's Ball*, a movie I had wanted to see since Halle Berry won an Academy Award for her lead role opposite Billy Bob Thornton.

At one point, while adjusting the volume, I got my foot tangled in the power cord. The loud crack of breaking wood was the first indication that something was awry. Then the left front leg of the antique dresser let go. The electrical cord of the television set tightened around my big toe as the dresser listed toward the corner of the errant leg.

Halle Berry turned into a hissing snowstorm of video nothingness.

The television toppled off the top of the dresser, its picture tube narrowly escaping impalement on the four-poster bed and vaporizing right in front of me. I'd never seen a television blow up and, at that instant,

between 'please Gods', my mind flashed through possible outcomes, all of which would be difficult to explain to Sheilah Carter Keeling.

Halle Berry was staring into the eyes of Billy Bob as the television ricocheted off the bedpost and jammed itself between the bed and the wall. The taut cable between the TV and the VCR catapulted the VCR unit across the room, turning Halle Berry into a hissing snowstorm of video nothingness. The dresser flopped onto its front just missing my naked foot.

It sounded like freight trains had collided in the dainty Red Rose suite at Glen Rose's Wild Rose Inn.

While vowing never again to try making a cozy B&B into a Holiday Inn, I nervously straightened up the mess and managed to glue the leg back on the dresser. To my amazement, the television and VCR still worked.

At breakfast, I asked Sheilah if she had heard the commotion the night before.

"No, dear. Why? What happened? Y'all have a party in there?" She asked innocently.

"Ahhh, errr. I'll send you a copy of my book," I offered, figuring I'd buy a little time.

25. Hot Times in the Mojave

The outside temperature display on the rearview mirror registered 116 degrees Fahrenheit. Our maxxed-out air conditioner was keeping things surprisingly cool inside but the sun load through the windshield felt like flames on my hands as I played the steering wheel, avoiding boulders and ruts gouged into the narrow track across a remote section of California's Mojave Desert.

The *Drive at Own Risk* sign, honeycombed with bullet holes, we passed an hour earlier had been a nice touch. When I opened the window, it felt like I was sticking my face into a gigantic pizza oven. Even the smatterings of scrubby desert bushes and hardy cacti seemed to be suffering.

To my right, the southern expanse of Death Valley shimmered on the

horizon like a ghostly mirage in a spaghetti western movie. We hadn't seen a sign of life for hours and the fuel gauge, hovering at just over a quarter tank, was swelling by the minute in my mind's eye.

Lisa and I were adamant about solving the last piece of a routing puzzle we were assembling for an upcoming driving event between Las Vegas and Morro Bay, on the Pacific coast midway between Los Angeles and San Francisco. We had driven a distance the equivalent of Toronto to Vancouver over California back roads in the previous week and, if we could find our way through the next 50 miles, we would have the basis of a workable program.

Questioning whether stubbornness was blind-siding common sense, I recalled the conversation with a road maintenance foreman we encountered before turning off the main road onto the desolate track.

"You can get to Death Valley by keeping right at a fork about 10 miles in. Go left and it takes you somewhere out there in the middle…" He seemed perplexed by our desire to find a short cut across that part of the sweltering Mojave Desert.

When I opened the window, it felt like I was sticking my face into a gigantic pizza oven.

It was my first drive in a Mitsubishi product and after pounding the rented all-wheel-drive Montero Sport SUV for the past seven days, my respect factor was high. It was peppy, comfortable and well-appointed. At first I felt guilty about the torture I was putting it through, but then I figured if it was in Alamo's rental fleet, they had to be prepared for people to use it in applications it was designed for. The torment was, in an adolescent way, my duty.

Lisa and I weren't talking much, just staring at the compass ensuring our direction jived with the desert map she was fixated on. To break the silence, I slipped in the only CD we had on board, *The Best of Buck Owens and His Buckaroos* that we had picked up at his show bar in Bakersfield the day before. Just one more go at *My Heart Skips a Beat* when the ominous sign appeared.

'CHINA LAKE NAVAL WEAPONS CENTER – LIVE BOMBING RANGE. DO NOT PASS THIS SIGN WITHOUT PERMISSION FROM THE INSTALLMENT COMMANDER'.

Our old friend, the bullet-riddled *Drive at own risk* warning sign, seemed rather docile as I visualized us getting vaporized out there in the Mojave Desert while Mr. Installment Commander tested a top-secret new weapon. I ejected Buck and his Buckaroos, turned around and headed back for the Death Valley fork.

Descending to the valley floor, we decided to drive to Ridgecrest, in the high desert just east of the Sequoia National Forest, where we could hole up for the night, chill out and reconsider our options. We passed the likes of Badwater, Devil's Golf Course, Devil's Cornfield and the improbable Furnace Creek Inn while watching the scorching fireball set behind Telescope Mountain. At 282 feet below sea level, even after sunset, the outside temperature was still over 104 degrees Fahrenheit.

About 10:00 p.m., we arrived in Ridgecrest, a forgettable place with

Even the smatterings of scrubby desert bushes and hardy cacti seemed to be suffering.

a string of motels and mangy-looking eateries. To our dismay, every accommodation in town was occupied except for a room with a broken air conditioner. We took it, foolishly reasoning the discomfort would be like a night at home during one of Halifax's rare heat waves.

A conglomeration of construction trucks was hogging the parking spaces in front of our room so we parked out front and lugged our bags into the sauna-like room. Too sweaty to make notes, I flicked every button on the TV remote to no avail. Bobby, the chatty receptionist, offered two more remotes that didn't work. Then finally through a series of mysterious gyrations, Lisa managed to turn on the television.

It was stuck on one station, a sci-fi network showing a movie about space men trapped on a sweltering red planet that looked like the Mojave Desert through a red filter. I finally drifted off well after midnight watching the original black and white version of *The Fly*.

Then at precisely 4:45 a.m., it started. The rattle of diesel trucks firing up in the parking lot snapped us out of our sticky sleep. The heat in the room was staggering. I was drenched in sweat and all I could think of was the air-conditioning knob on the dash of the Montero.

In my haste to escape the inferno I accidentally ripped the security lock off the door. Then an unexpected blast of chilly dry air hit me in the face. "Duuuh", I thought, remembering those geography lessons about cold nights in hot deserts.

"Losers." I heard Lisa mutter. "Let's get the Montero's heater fired up."

26. Road Fever Rerun

I awoke covered in sweat, feeling feverish and scared. As I tried to determine my whereabouts, a series of loud bangs caught my attention. I had heard plenty of electronic buzzes, beeps and squawks during the previous few days but there was something very different going on now. Between bangs I could hear laughter, mature at times, but mostly from young people.

Those previous noises had been generated in my room at Brookwood Medical Center in Birmingham, Alabama, where I had been under observation during a bout with an exotic and stubborn 'flu strain. Although not quite the relaxation I would have wanted, the competent medical staff had extended ample southern hospitality during their barrage of medicating, testing and questioning. All the while my body temperature fluctuated like the temperature gauge on a K-car towing an Airstream travel trailer over the Rocky Mountains in mid-July.

But now there was no hospital smell. I could feel a soft duvet on my chest. Birds chirped while a cool breeze blew across my face. The room was so bright I had a hard time opening my eyes. Then I heaved a sigh

During recovery, which was surprisingly quick, I was subdued by the thought of my fragility and how abruptly things had turned from normal to desperate.

My body temperature fluctuated like the temperature gauge on a K-car towing an Airstream travel trailer over the Rocky Mountains in mid-July.

of relief, realizing the suspected fever was actually the heat of the sun shining through the huge open bedroom window at Dell and Carolyn Hill's Selwood Farm. I had gone to the private hunting preserve, an hour's drive east of Birmingham, to convalesce for the weekend after my semi-delirious visit to Brookwood Medical Center.

Focusing on the scene out the window, I realized the banging sound was coming from a group of people shooting at clay 'pigeons' that a half dozen mechanical gizmos were flinging across an open field.

"Pull!" Twang… Bang… Bang, Bang!! Laughter, more shouts of "Pull!", more bangs. They were obviously having a good time.

Although being sick on the road is far from my idea of a good time, I was happy to hear someone was having fun out there. But, feeling weak and disoriented, I just wanted to be home.

I have been lucky when it comes to illness away from home though. There have been episodes with a rebellious digestive system, sore throats and the odd toothache. But, aside from this Alabama incident there has only been one time where I felt things were spinning out of control.

In 1997, on the eve of Pakistan's celebration of 50 years of independence, Lisa and I found ourselves in the Marriott Hotel in the port of Karachi. We were preparing for meetings to determine safe and expeditious transit routes through Pakistan for an upcoming bid to establish a new around-the-world driving record.

Since the next day was a holiday, I thought it would be a good time to send a newsletter to recipients on our mailing list, about 350 of them. Obviously, they would enjoy a letter from Pakistan postmarked on its 50th anniversary. After writing the letter, Lisa and I went to a nearby bazaar and bought envelopes as well as the biggest postage stamps we could find to decorate them.

That night while watching festivities on the streets below from our white-on-white hotel suite, Lisa stuffed envelopes while I licked more than 300 postage stamps. Lisa reminded me of a *Seinfeld* episode where one of the characters dies after poisoning herself by licking discounted envelopes.

"Oh, that was just a TV program!" I scoffed.

By midnight, the jubilation below had abated and we were staring at a fine stack of stamped and sealed newsletters that I felt would be an exotic addition to any mailbox. So with a thick, gluey-tasting tongue, I retired.

A few hours later, the process of ejecting the Pakistani stamp glue from my body commenced so violently that, by daybreak, I thought I was losing consciousness. It seemed ironic that after everything I'd been through, I was finally going to be brought down by a newsletter mailing.

Fortunately Lisa tracked down the hotel's in-house doctor who administered an injection, enabling me to keep down oral medication, reversing the out-of-control situation into which I had deteriorated. During recovery, which was surprisingly quick, I was subdued by the thought of my fragility and how abruptly things had turned from normal to desperate.

The Alabama experience had many of the elements of the Karachi stint. It was sudden, surprising and I could feel myself slipping to a level where I quickly needed medical help. Thankfully, I was close to a respectable medical facility.

Lying in the hospital room watching the clock provided plenty of time to think about what may have fueled my downward spiral. Forty-eight straight workdays with a ridiculous level of sleep deprivation. Changing hotels almost every day. Constant problem-solving, unrelenting deadlines and an I-can-do-anything attitude.

The convalescence also gave me time to feel sorry for myself. Poor me, I missed a few days work. Poor me, I can't do my power-walk today. Poor me, I'll probably still feel weak for another few days.

I looked out the window of Dell and Carolyn's guesthouse. The open meadows surrounded by tall graceful pines and distant oak trees looked fluorescent in the spring sunshine. The shooting was still going on. So was the laughter and sense of excitement.

Then, as I focused my gaze on the shooting stands, I noticed something that made my self-pity seem rather overblown.

All of the shooters were sitting in wheelchairs.

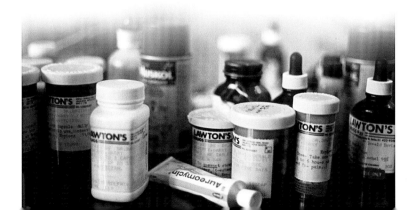

27. Elements of a Texas Road Challenge

"Don't forget, this load included a La-Z-Boy armchair, an antique Underwood typewriter and an 80s vintage cash register along with this plastic replica of an ancient Greek clock." I tried to keep a straight face as I displayed the flimsy fake-gold timepiece.

A healthy applause ricocheted around the room full of journalists and Honda Motor Company executives. We were in the final stages of judging to determine the most unusual, awkward or bizarre $20 object participants in the *The Great Canadian Elemental Media Challenge* could pack into their new Honda Element vehicles.

"Now what about this?" I held it high by the left leg. A roar came from the audience. Then cat calls, whistles and applause that sounded like

Welcome to Hico, Texas where Everybody is either a Somebody or Billy the Kid!

frenzied country music fans seeking an encore at a Shania Twain concert.

There was no doubt, the lower half of the plaster mannequin was a hands-down winner. I invited Pierre Michaud and Eric LeFrancois to the front and asked the circumstances of their purchase.

"Without the top half, the antique shop thought they would never sell it," laughed Eric.

More cheers from the crowd that was spread out in the comfortable dining room of the Rough Creek Lodge near the town of Glen Rose in central Texas.

On the table behind me, items representing other competitors' purchases were on display. An intriguing fossil, a tacky Texan wall hanging and a tuft of hay from the four bales one team had stuffed into their Element had already undergone scrutiny from the audience. A musty, powder-blue corduroy cushion, from the hide-a-bed the *Urban Male* magazine team had maneuvered between the Element's flip-up rear seats, had drawn a lively response.

The Challenge was comprised of four scoring elements in which two-person crews road-tripped over remote Texan country roads in an effort to rack up points for a variety of tasks.

Participants were provided maps to 23 scoring sites between Rough Creek Lodge, a two-hour drive southwest of Dallas, and Linda's Café, an unpretentious, homey restaurant in tiny Gustine. At the scoring sites, teams completed assignments ranging from identifying sale items in a store window to classifying dinosaurs tangling in a mural at the Visitor's Centre in Dinosaur Valley State Park. They checked out the stars on Stephenville's Cowboy Capital Walk of Fame. They visited a place called Fairy.

After repeating 'Pretty Peggy Pepper' quickly 3 times to the staff at the Dr Pepper Bottling Plant in Dublin, Texas, they were told that only Dublin Dr Pepper still utilizes pure cane sugar, rather than corn syrup, in its recipe. They wandered through the Billy the Kid Museum, learned that *Everybody is a Somebody* in Hico and discovered that 9 drops of the secret ingredient goes into the phosphate drinks at the soda fountain in Hamilton's Jordan Pharmacy.

At Glen Rose's Wild Rose Inn, Sheilah Carter Keeling confessed to inquiring journalists that she met Elvis Presley on a ship crossing the

18. A "double-take-down" meal is one that is:
   a. very expensive
   b. very good
   c. results in expulsion at both ends
   d. comes with super-sized fries

19. The official vegetable of Texas is:
   a. the parsnip
   b. the sweet onion
   c. the broccoli
   d. the jicama

20. Which one of these Texas laws is NOT in effect?
   a. It is illegal to drive without windshield wipers
   b. It is illegal to shoot a buffalo from the 4th storey of a hotel *2nd storey*
   c. It is illegal to milk another person's cow
   d. It is illegal to walk barefoot without first obtaining a special five-dollar permit

Atlantic when she was a teenager. A section of the Rally called *The Bridges of Hamilton County* took participants over a maze of dusty backroads in search of 5 rickety, and in some cases non-existent, bridges.

Teams received disposable cameras to snap items en route that started with the letters E-L-E-M-E-N-T. Points were awarded for finding enough friendly Texans to fill the seats of their Elements. Two Texans on the tailgate captured on film and photographing barbershops through the side cargo doors beefed up their scores as well.

While the road game was in progress, Challengers vied for the 'Egghead Award' by attempting to answer 20 Texas trivia questions. After all, every visitor to the Lone Star State should know that it is illegal to shoot buffalo from the 2nd storey of a hotel.

At the end of the day, scoring the rally and the trivia test were straightforward. Being a former school teacher, Lisa was in her element with a red corrector pen. Peter Schlay, our medic, whose only emergency was treating himself for what turned out to be a broken foot, added scores. Meanwhile, our technician, Bill Rumsey whisked the film from the cameras to nearby Stephenville for processing so we could score the photo contest.

When Bill returned with the participants' photographs, agreeing on the best overall image wasn't so easy. Would it be a beauty shot, an action photo or a snapshot that would encompass the spirit of what had just

Opposite page, top: Half-man, half-mannequin, Pierre Michaud took home the prize for most bizarre $20-object.

transpired on the backroads of central Texas?

We settled on a shot of two hefty geezers sitting on the tailgate of the Element, evidently weighing well over the 199 kilogram load limit. The construction workers that Paul Williams and Richard Russell had cajoled into posing on the tailgate symbolized the good-natured way just about all the rural Texans had reacted to the Canadian visitors' quest.

The overall winners of the *The Great Canadian Elemental Media Challenge* were Ted Laturnus and Lawrence Yap with a total score of 234 of a possible 265 points. Road warriors *extraordinaires*!

The next morning, everyone was transported to the Dallas-Fort Worth Airport for their flights back to Canada. I wandered around the Lodge. It truly was an impressive work of architecture filled with tasteful Texan artifacts. I looked across the dining room where the awards banquet had been held. Most of the items from the $20-load display were gone, back to Canada as souvenirs perhaps.

But the half-mannequin was still there, sprawled across a table. I wasn't surprised. It would have been a tough go at Canada Customs.

"Anything to declare?"

"Half of a *what*?"

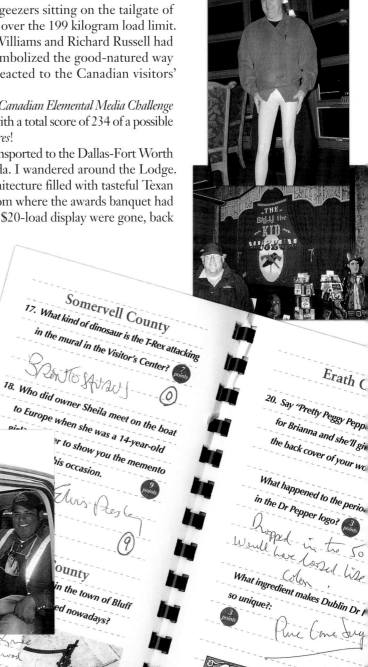

Somervell County

17. What kind of dinosaur is the T-Rex attacking in the mural in the Visitor's Center? *7 points*

BRONTOSAURUS — ⓪

18. Who did owner Sheila meet on the boat to Europe when she was a 14-year-old ...r to show you the memento ...his occasion. *9 points*

Elvis Presley

⑨

...ounty

...n the town of Bluff ...ed nowadays?

Erath C...

20. Say "Pretty Peggy Pepp... for Brianna and she'll gi... the back cover of your wo...

What happened to the perio... in the Dr Pepper logo? *3 points*

Dropped — in the 50... Would have looked like... Colon.

What ingredient makes Dublin Dr P... so unique?: *3 points*

Pure Cane Sug...

rail wood
Used in America...

28. Multiple Choice Baja

After drifting luxuriously on houseboats, enduring seven physical challenges and driving 800 miles in 55 hours, the participants were hooked on life in the fast lane.

I pushed the throttles until both tachometers hovered around the 4500 RPM redlines. Nothing budged so I eased them forward until they read 5500 RPM. Still nothing.

It was at that instant I visualized our ambitious plan coming to an unceremonious halt with the bulk of it yet to unfold. Desperate, I asked the four on-board journalists to move to the rear deck of the 65-foot houseboat I was trying to get off the beach of Lake Mohave, a bulge of the Colorado River on the Nevada - Arizona border 25 miles downstream from the Hoover Dam.

"Get as far back on the quarterdeck as you can!" I shouted over the roar, hoping the shift in weight would alter the centre of gravity enough for the two 175-horsepower engines to drag us off the beach and keep Subaru's *Baja Multiple Choice Adventure* on track.

The massive hull finally moved a few inches then slid out into the calm early-morning waters. I watched three more of the huge boats struggle off the beach like a fortunate pod of beached beluga whales. Judging by the cackle on the 2-way radio, their crews seemed as relieved as I was to be launched.

It was the beginning of the second day of a three-day driving adventure for a group of lifestyle journalists between Las Vegas and Morro Bay, a bustling fishing town on the California coast midway between Los Angeles and San Francisco.

In the previous three weeks, Lisa and I had logged the equivalent of two equator lengths on flights across North America. We had driven more than 5,000 miles of Southern California backroads checking out 160 hotels, restaurants and attractions to find the right 23 venues to make a viable trial for participants and the new Subaru Baja vehicles they would be driving.

Prior to launching the awkward, floating behemoths, our guests had already connected a few of the dots on the *Baja Multiple Choice Adventure*. Within an hour of landing in Las Vegas, they had dangled from cliffs as tall as a 30-storey building under the watchful eye of Laura Grandstaff's *Sky's the Limit* climbers in the stunning Red Rocks Canyon. They had driven to the base of the Hoover Dam and then rafted down the awesome Colorado River. After a rendezvous with speed boats, the final leg took them to luxurious houseboats moored on a remote stretch of beach. Later, under a canopy of starlight, they feasted on rustic Tuscan bean soup, grilled fillet tenderloins and fresh lobster. Tales of self-discovery were rampant.

Behind the scenes, Lisa and our support staff, Bill Rumsey and Peter Schlay, juggled a logistical Rubic's cube of speedboats, kayaks, houseboats, support vehicles and the 5 Baja event vehicles. Spare moments were spent wracking our brains developing a series of exams which we handed out every night to check up on what the participants had learned, with multiple-choice answers of course.

In the morning, after coaxing the houseboats off the beach, they piloted the armada down Lake Mohave for an hour before slipping into kayaks and racing into the marina where their Bajas awaited. A quick drive briefing sent them on their way into the Mojave National Preserve for a hike break at Hole-in-the-Wall, aptly named by 18th-century ranchers in hot pursuit of cattle rustlers who seemingly disappeared into the rugged canyon walls, bovine booty and all.

The next two days unfolded according to plan. Participants feasted at the unlikely Mad Greek Café in Baker, wandered the deserted streets of Randsburg Ghost Town and descended 4,000 feet on mountain bikes led by John Stallone's *Mountain and River Adventurers* in the Southern Sierra Nevada Range. A lunch stop at Wool Growers Restaurant in Bakersfield, California let them rub shoulders with eclectic locals over a 'Soup and Salad Set-up' lunch.

The energized gaggle of drivers finally nosed their dusty Bajas through the oil fields and cotton plantations of the fertile San Joaquin Valley into Morro Bay. During their late afternoon surfing session among the sea

lions and pelicans, our crew finally had a chance to pause.

With seven physical challenges and 800 miles of driving in 55 hours, the participants were raving about life in the fast lane. The Bajas had taken abusive desert tracks and twisty mountain routes in stride. Aside from a scraped knee after a mountain bike wipe-out, there had been no injury and our 50-balls-in-the-air logistical plan had looked like a well-executed chess game to everyone involved.

The next night, after we had ferried everyone to the airport for their trips home, Lisa, Pete, Bill and I relaxed over dinner at a beach side restaurant.

I told them about my terror with the over-revved houseboat engines on the shore of Lake Mohave. It seemed like months ago. I asked Bill if he had had a moment of doubt.

"When I woke up that morning on the houseboats and thought about their dashboards and engine controls," he confessed, "I had a knot in my stomach all right. 'Cause I thought we'd never even get the engines started."

I thanked him for keeping that knot to himself.

29. High Speed Hi-Jinks

At the end of the straight-away, I considered easing up on the throttle but figured the 33-degree banked corner on the world's fastest speedway would handle the 115 miles per hour I was driving. After all, competition cars regularly drive in excess of 180 mph on this track.

I held it down and took the turn with surprising ease in the high outside lane. Up there, more than 45 feet above the bottom of the track, the photographer shooting my pass looked very small. But there were no spectators in the race world's longest bleachers and no other cars tearing around Talledega Super Speedway with me. The pits were empty. There were no national TV cameras or concession stands selling hot dogs and souvenirs either. Just me with a wedged grin in my unlikely ride, a 2003 Subaru Forester, that was handling surprisingly well.

A few weeks earlier, Lisa and I had been asked to produce the drive portion of the North American media introduction for the redesigned 2003 Subaru Forester. Alabama was chosen as a location for a number of reasons. An early spring and neighbourly people along with Alabama's relatively central continental location were attractive elements for consideration. The tough, trendy Foresters could be put through their paces over a variety of roads in and around the Talledega National Forest. Foresters in the Forest? Why not!

We had arranged for the lunch break at the Talledega Super Speedway where the guests would get a chance to run the Foresters on the track for a few laps. Since the scenario also included areas for acceleration and obstacle avoidance demonstrations, participants would get a good feel for the handling characteristics of the cars.

As I pushed the Forester around the 2.6-mile track, I thought of how my own motoring activities have provided many opportunities on the open road. But, aside from two *Cannonball One Lap of America* events and as many Alcan 5000 rallies, I have had very little experience in organized motorsports.

The new Subaru Forester was an unlikely yet agile ride on the world's fastest speedway.

In the 1960s, I would go to the 1/4-mile drag races which were held at an abandoned airstrip near Moncton, New Brunswick. Since twin Larry and I were in our early teens, we tagged along with older brother Bruce in our father's '63 Mercury Custom Monterey. To save money, Larry and I would stuff ourselves into the trunk a few miles before the ticket booth and stay there until Bruce reached the parking area down a deserted taxiway.

"Hey! There's Al Melanson in the next lane!" I'd hear one of Bruce's cronies yell over rumbling dual exhaust under the trunk floor. Then I'd hear the racket of burning rubber as Al lit up the tires. Even with a 300-horse 390 engine, the Merc was no match for Al's 409 Pontiac. It was a noisy tear down that taxiway.

The only other time I had a car on a track was during a summer high school job at a Mercury Lincoln dealership where I cleaned cars and kept the 'lot' presentable. Lloyd, the other 'lot boy', and I knew the local go-cart track at a deserted gravel pit was never used during the week. Sometimes at lunch, we would take a unit off the used car lot and head out to the gravel pit.

Lloyd Broad sheepishly contemplates extraction techniques after drifting the Beetle off the go-kart track.

Between egg sandwiches, we ran those mid-60s Anglias, Cortinas and VW Beetles flat out around that track. It was a lot of fun screeching around in those low key imports until Lloyd drifted a Beetle into a bunch of alder bushes and we had to go back to the dealership and sneak the tow truck to pull it back onto the track.

Those years brought me the closest I ever came to actual track racing. Larry and I bought a 1960 Ford for $25, knocked the windows out of it and entered it in a demolition derby. I figured, with a long trunk and a good reverse gear, I could destroy most of the competition by driving the big Ford backwards. But the afternoon before the race, my older brother crashed his MG and broke his leg so my parents put the brakes on my racing debut.

Back at the Talladega Speedway, I continued my laps for the photographer, holding the throttle flat on the floor until my leg ached. At 115 mph, there was not a lot of time to look around. I couldn't imagine what it would be like doing almost twice that speed hemmed in by up to 40 other NASCAR competitors.

Although I'll never have that kind of experience in front of 150,000 race fans, it was a treat to drive on the world's fastest race track for a while.

And the fact that I didn't have to crawl into the trunk of a '63 Mercury to get past the ticket booth made it even better.

30. *Big Screen Bile Attack*

I was standing on 59th Street in New York City in sweltering heat. Lisa rested a clammy hand on my shoulder while a bead of nervous sweat dripped down my face.

Every Boy Scout knot I used to know, from a sheepshank to a round-turn-and-two-and-a-half-hitches, tightened in the pit of my stomach. Lisa had an I-want-to-go-home look on her face as she stared at the commotion on the other side of the street.

It wasn't the pulse of the concrete jungle or a Central Park wilding that was getting to us. The source of our bile attack was the milling crowd in front of the Clearview Cinema with *New York International Film Festival* plastered across its marquee.

You HAVE TO PAY NOW OR GO TO JAIL!

"No points for plywood deer"

It was approaching two o'clock in the afternoon which was precisely the time when *No Borders*, the 50-minute documentary film we had worked on for 3 years, would be screened in front of the waiting throng. From our vantage point, the expectant patrons seemed like a serious lot. And the slate of competitive films like *Broke Even*, *Pay the Price* and *A Life Worth Living* did little to ease our apprehension.

Even though *No Borders* had recently won an award for Creative Excellence at the *U.S. International Independent Film and Video Festival* in Chicago, this would be the first time Lisa and I would view the film in the presence of more than a couple of relatives who were blood-bound to sit through it and react. We were literally minutes away from the Big Screen in the Big Apple with a theatre full of film festival groupies.

No going back. We wiped our brows, donned our hippest, grooviest attitudes and crossed the street. The doors opened, tickets were collected and the crowd gathered around the concession stand. This was the real thing - popcorn and all.

Lisa and I walked stone-faced past the concession stand, figuring licorice and Smarties wouldn't be a good idea considering the condition of our stomachs.

"What if they don't laugh at the funny parts?" I nervously whispered to Lisa.

"What if they leave after it starts?" she replied.

As we settled into our seats, my heart was pounding so hard I thought the buttons on my shirt would pop off. Then, that familiar music we had heard so many late nights during post-production at Jeff Fish's editing suite back in Halifax blasted through the theatre like an old friend coming to our rescue.

Panoramic opening scenes from Calcutta, Istanbul and Tuva filled the huge silver screen. I cringed when my twangy, nasal voice narrated the first few minutes outlining the 14-day driving adventure upon which ten couples from as many countries were about to embark.

The audience was quiet as they were introduced to a Turkish palace renovator, a Canadian billiards supply mogul, a Tuvan throat singer and a Mexican race car driver. As scenes of a French chiropractor, a Guatemalan school teacher and an Israeli fashion designer flashed across the screen, sound bites of their accents provided the feel of an international 'who-dunnit?' flick.

AURORA IN FRONT OF THE FAAABULOUS LUXOR PYRAMID VIVA LAS VEGAS 5:30 AM 10/5

The cosmopolitan Vacation Challengers, hailing from far-flung locales, snapped Polaroids of roadside Americana and taped them into their trip logbooks.

During production, we had worried that the information load at the beginning of the film was where we might loose some of the audience. But they seemed hooked on every detail as the concept played itself out in the opening scenes. Detroit to Beverly Hills. Two weeks on the road armed with new V-8 Oldsmobile Auroras, bags full of travel accessories and a list of 500 en route attractions. At six lavish en route dinner parties, competitors boasted of their exploits and plotted strategies for the next leg in their bids to out-vacation each other.

When Bulent Güngor of Team Turkey explained how his wife Merih had turned white when a Michigan state trooper handed him a $400 speeding ticket, the audience broke up. When Team India's Saloo Choudhury talked about the dirty look he received from Team Guatemala as he passed their car – another round of laughter.

And when a participant hypothesized that the majestically carved Mount Rushmore was "…more impressive actually here than when you see it on TV", the audience lost it.

It seemed apparent to the spectators that the tale of international camaraderie with a touch of road gonzo was well worth sitting through. That had been our intent in producing the film and the reaction of the audience was making Lisa and I finally relax.

WARNING

NATIONAL PARK SERVICE

MANY VISITORS HAVE BEEN GORED BY BUFFALO

BUFFALO CAN WEIGH 2000 POUNDS AND CAN SPRINT AT 30 MPH, THREE TIMES FASTER THAN YOU CAN RUN

THESE ANIMALS MAY APPEAR TAME BUT ARE WILD, UNPREDICTABLE, AND DANGEROUS

DO NOT APPROACH BUFFALO

Get Your Modems Running…!

Entering Aurora Vacation Challenge

ILLINOIS

FT. SHERIDAN
CHICAGO
BLACKHAWK STATE PARK
URBANA (of U. of I.)
NEW SALEM STATE PARK
SPRINGFIELD (LINCOLN TOMB)
COAL FIELDS

THE HOME OF LINCOLN

112

CONTINENTAL DIVIDE ELEV 9658

Aside from a good ol' American road trip, the film focused on the rendezvous activities at an upscale fishing camp, a lush golf resort, an eclectic dude ranch and even the rambling estate where former U.S. President Ronald Reagan had gotten married.

The Vacation Challengers delighted the audience as they swapped stories of backroads and bar rooms, of imposters and exotic dancers, state troopers and rustic geezers.

Some got lost. A few got cranky. But in the end, it was the spectacular sights unfolding through their windshields and the memorable roadside encounters that glued the unlikely competitors, and the film, together.

As the credits rolled, there was heartening applause. Dregs of laughter were still erupting when the house lights came up.

Then, as Lisa and I got ready to slip out of the theatre, we heard it from somewhere out in the audience.

"Are the film makers in the house?"

The receptive film audience soaked up the 16-day vacation adventure motoring from Detroit to Los Angeles.

NO BORDERS produced and directed by GARRY SOWERBY & LISA CALVI
editor JEFF FISH • videography JERRY VIENNEAU • story consultant JOHN DEMONT
original music by KURT HAHN • sound mixer CHUCK O'HARA • graphics MICHAEL DOYLE
research HELEN MACMILLAN • post production facility OCEAN DIGITAL
© 2000 • www.adventuredrive.ca
...TED • Halifax, Nova Scotia, CANADA
...il. odyssey@hfx.eastlink.ca

Chapter 5 The Blur of Woods and Rock

The cooking oil went on a rampage, smashing three plastic glasses before dumping itself on a wandering roll of toilet paper.

31. Riding the Rails

I used the grab handles to pull myself up into the cab. It had an industrial grey no-nonsense interior. I slipped behind the steering wheel, which was flat, like one you would find on a Greyhound bus. Floor level was higher than the roof of the Honda Accord parked beside me.

Out the massive windshield, the street ahead looked impossibly narrow and when I leaned out the window to adjust the side mirror, I could see those rear frame rails. No box. Only frame rails that went on forever with four huge tires way back there holding them up.

"This is definitely a lot of machinery," I muttered, as I turned the key and fired up the Caterpillar diesel sitting under the cab.

The rumble of that Cat made me grin. But when I thought about what lay ahead, a huge butterfly cranked through my stomach. Thirty-five

hundred kilometres of driving between Calgary and Toronto in this T-7500 GMC tilt chassis-cab was about to give me a three-day look at a world three metres above the pavement. A place where everyone is working, because people that high off the road are usually pulling, pushing or carrying something that is heavy, big or dangerous.

A contact had told me about a medium duty truck chassis-cab that had to be driven from Calgary to Toronto. I jumped at the chance. Up there, in a big rig, checking out what was happening on the road between Alberta and southern Ontario seemed like quite an opportunity.

Before I left, temporary mudflaps were strapped to the framerails behind the back wheels… a pine board with what looked like two strips of doormat hanging from it.

With a combined closing speed of about 200 km/h, the relationship is brief. Just time for a nod, wave or a shrug even.

On the road it was 2400 RPMs in 6th gear. One hundred and four kilometres per hour. It was fairly quiet in there but the ride was rough. With no weight on the back, my body was doomed to flop out the rhythm of every pavement crack and surface irregularity between Cowtown and Hogtown. Tuning radio channels on the move was out of the question so I implemented the 'get-a-tape-at-every-stop' rule. The first opportunity was near the Saskatchewan border where I found Merle Haggard's *Super Hits Volume 3. Workin' Man Blues* right there on the back cover.

There's something about country music, especially the old stuff, when you're trapped in a vehicle for a few days en route a destination so far away you can't imagine ever getting there. The words to those tearjerkers get you down the road. Relate them to life experiences. Admit you were in love with that 'purdy young daughter' up there on Wolverton Mountain. Listen to *Flowers on the Wall* 10 times. Play it over and over again, no one will know. A chance to figure out all those words you never understood and were too ashamed to ask anyone.

I sat tall in the saddle through Medicine Hat and Swift Current then stopped for the night in Moose Jaw. In the morning I knew what I was going to do all day. Head east!

I pumped the air seat up another six inches, just enough for a height advantage over the attractive redhead in the Kenworth at a traffic light in Brandon, Manitoba. I was surprised how many women were out there running big rigs.

A bruised afternoon sky over Winnipeg

silhouetted flocks of Canada Geese beating their way across the horizon. I was in full driving bliss. The panorama unfolding beyond my big-screen windshield made me realize what a lucky man I was… the view, the height, the solitude. I fantasized about buying one of these trucks and putting my office on the back of it. The wife would love it out there filling up the back yard tethered to the house while I waited for an excuse to take it somewhere.

In the woods of eastern Manitoba I thought about responsibility. Throttle response, brake feel and sound were constant reminders to respect this vehicle. Once I forgot the size factor and almost clipped the back of a military tank transporter I was maneuvering around at a fuel stop.

With no cellular phone service between Thunder Bay and Sault Ste. Marie, I settled into 800 kilometres of incommunicado. No more talking to people sounding like I was strapped to an electric paint mixer… "Aaaaaand hhhhhow aaaaare yyyyyyou?"

From my elevated vantage point, there was a lot to see. Stunning scenery and plenty of car roofs. Roof racks. Roof antenna. At eye level, it was the eyes of the people doing exactly what I was doing, moving a big hunk of machinery down the road.

With a combined closing speed of about 200 km/h, the relationship is brief. Just time for a nod, wave or a shrug even. An acknowledgment

The panorama unfolding beyond my big-screen windshield made me realize what a lucky man I was… the view, the height, the solitude.

that we're kin of some sort. Most of the other drivers instigated the waves. I began to suspect I was a slackard. Or were they sympathy waves?

"Here comes a poor sod in a cab-chassis. He deserves a wave."

There were lots of places where truckers could check their loads. I'd pull off once in a while to check mine; a couple of dangling door mats back there on the frame rails. I tried to avoid weigh scales where I got bored looks.

"Keep movin', boy."

In Sault Ste. Marie, the cell phone came to life. It was Monday morning and my normal world was waiting. I hated the thought of it all ending.

By the time I headed south from Sudbury for the last few hundred kilometres, I felt like Bill Murray in the movie Groundhog Day, who wakes up every morning to exactly the same routine.

Just north of Toronto, I called Cheryl Kitchen, my contact at Shaw GMC in Calgary.

"Hi Garry, you're in Toronto?" she seemed surprised that I was there already.

"Yyyyyyyes, it's bbbeeen qqqqquite a tttttttttrrrip," I croaked.

"The other one is ready. When will you be back for it?" she laughed.

"I'm ooon tttttthe aaaafternoon fffffflight."

I chuckled at the thought of doing it all over again.

Caterpillar diesel powered
GMC T-7500 Chassis Cab

32. *Serendipitous Vibrations of a Superior Nature*

The delicate but flamboyant table setting was what you would expect in an uptown, fine dining eatery in Toronto, Chicago or even New York. Although not extensive, the dinner menu boasted the likes of shrimp a la grecque, rack of lamb and a scallop concoction that sounded divine. The prime rib roast I had eaten the night before was to die for.

Mary Burnett, who owns and operates the unlikely Serendipity Gardens Café, effortlessly made Lisa and I feel like special friends as we relaxed over breakfast. Quiet music in synch with soft sunlight slinking over the table complemented our comatose sleep in the cozy four-room guest house a short distance away that Mary's partner, Roger Alty, had built himself. Roger and Mary knew how to create ambience, they were engaging raconteurs and they certainly knew how to make people comfortable.

One look out the plate glass window beside our table quickly dissolved the trendy uptown illusion as a howling wind churned up the dregs of the overnight dusting of snow. In the distance the looming silhouette of Quay

Serendipity led us to tiny Rossport, Ontario.

Island dwarfed a rustic boat dock and two lonely ice fishing huts, barely visible through snow blowing across the frozen northern fringe of mighty Lake Superior. Without doubt, the Serendipity Gardens Café and Guesthouse in tiny Rossport, Ontario is guaranteed to live up to its name for travellers driving the lonely stretch of Trans Canada Highway between Sault Ste. Marie and Thunder Bay.

I've driven that route dozens of times since first venturing across Canada in 1971 in my new Datsun 240Z. But my obsession was always to get through the 700 kilometres of two-lane blacktop as quickly as possible. Those hours held hostage to the blur of woods and rock, punctuated with a smattering of road signs proclaiming hard-to-pronounce villages, seemed a waste of time.

Lake Superior, unpredictable and desolate, was usually not visible since I tried to schedule the transit as an all-nighter. It was a place to make up time during cross-country junkets.

But all that changed while developing the plan for the media launch for the new Pontiac Vibe, which was to be presented live on the Internet through a 17-day cross-country driving trek from Halifax to Vancouver. Since the program would allow media entrants to score points for experiencing the roadside lifeblood of Canada, Lisa and I had to slow down and get into search mode for unusual and bizarre quirks of Canadian lore.

Participants would experience the real Canada: the blizzards, the potholes, the people in the little towns and the culture. They would

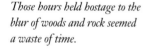

Those hours held hostage to the blur of woods and rock seemed a waste of time.

sample an old-fashioned way of travelling when getting from point A to point B meant coming into contact with a lot of stuff in between.

Our research revealed plenty of things to see and ponder along the shores of Lake Superior. The 'Goose' at Wawa erected to overlook the first traffic over the top of Superior, has somehow evolved into three strategically placed Geese. Press a button and the original gives its life story, although I'd like to know why a goose named Al has a female voice. Up the road, a plaque identifies the midpoint of the Trans Canada Highway. Halfway along the east coast of Superior, the town of White River is home to Winnie the Pooh. Across from Pooh Park, the friendly staff at Louis's Place restaurant serves the best pie anyone could ask for.

There are plenty of stunning vistas to gaze out over the largest fresh water lake in the world and get a chill thinking about Gordon Lightfoot's moving ballad about the wreck of the Edmund Fitzgerald, an ore carrier that sank in those storm-prone waters. We learned of prisoner-of-war camps that dotted the coast during the Second World War and tried to imagine the misery of escapees attempting to make their way out of the desolation.

With very little cellular phone service, the drive is a good place to get out of touch making it more of a holiday rather than a lost day. Two hours east of Thunder Bay, a five-minute diversion to Red Rock places travellers on the doorsteps of the Red Rock Inn, the immaculately-restored officers quarters of one of the area's former prisoner-of-war camps.

If you are heading west approaching Thunder Bay, any feelings of accomplishment are nullified at the mind-numbing moment when you see the statue of Terry Fox, erected where he was forced to stop his cross-Canada fundraising run for cancer research.

But after a few days immersed in the history and sights of the drive between Sault Ste. Marie and Thunder Bay, one thing became very clear. The next time I drive the Superior route, I'll make sure to eat at Mary and Roger's Serendipity Gardens Café and hopefully beat the lines waiting to overnight in their guest house.

With only four rooms, it will not be long before more people have a Serendipitous experience and realize there's a slice of uptown very far out of town in funky Rossport.

Any feelings of accomplishment are nullified at the mind-numbing moment when you see the statue of Terry Fox, erected where he was forced to stop his cross-Canada fundraising run for cancer research.

33. Labrador Vacation

The silence was broken by what sounded like the report of a high-powered rifle. My eyes flashed to the left side mirror. Smoke was everywhere, but I told myself it was from the forest fires that had been burning for weeks. It could have been one of eight tires rupturing on the coarse gravel road, but everything seemed to be tracking properly - none of the usual wobble or sway associated with a blowout. I hit the four-way flashers and eased on the brakes. The motorhome in front of us disappeared into the thick haze.

In the seconds following, the noise evolved into a discordant symphony of thwacking sounds, accompanied by a continuous high-pitched hiss. I focused on a black hose thrashing wildly between my GMC Jimmy and the 8-metre Airstream travel trailer hooked to the rear. One end was still

Ron didn't hear. He was already halfway out the door, scrambling for the valve that would pacify the berserk serpent.

attached to a propane tank mounted on the Airstream, but the other end was spraying highly volatile propane gas into an atmosphere already choked with smoke.

We were just about stopped. As I steered to the shoulder of the road my left hand found the door handle.

"Let's get that valve closed!" I yelled across the seat to Ron King, a journalist from Knoxville, Tennessee, who was travelling with me.

Ron didn't hear. He was already halfway out the door, scrambling for the valve that would pacify the berserk serpent. A new Caddy towing a tandem U-Haul drifted by and almost clipped my open door. I watched the words 'Adventure in Moving' vanish into the opaque smoke ahead just as Ron twisted the propane valve shut. The ruptured hose lay limp against the tailgate. The ashen-faced writer was shaking when he got back in the truck.

"Nice vacation," he gasped. "Let's roll, or we'll never catch the convoy."

After we cleared the forest fires, it was still a long way through the wilderness to Labrador City.

****

Most people take vacations at one time or another. If they're looking for a little adventure, unusual wildlife or virgin terrain, they sometimes head for exotic locales far away from home.

For most of my adult life, my business has involved getting motor vehicles to and from the distant corners of the planet for one reason or another. After a series of far-flung adventures, a local endeavor seemed to make good sense so I decided to take a trip closer to my home in Nova Scotia. It would be a vacation of sorts.

The trip was conceived during a conversation with a retired accountant who told me of his dream to drive to Goose Bay, Labrador from the Province of Quebec. He explained that the road dead-ended at a railway line about 50 kilometres east of Labrador City - 500 kilometres short of his goal. He had made it that far on two separate occasions.

The idea percolated and I began researching an area that was, relatively speaking, right in my own backyard. I had learned the basics in grade school geography. Newfoundland and Labrador make up one province divided into two distinct parts. Labrador is located on the northeast tip of Canada's mainland, bordered by Quebec along the west and south.

Separated by the Strait of Belle Isle, Newfoundland stands alone in the North Atlantic.

Labrador is a sparsely populated wilderness with a few fishing villages on the southeast coast and mining in the northwest interior. Caribou outnumber people by more than 80 to one. Many of its hunting and fishing lodges and small communities can only be reached by airplanes or coastal ferries, and until recently there wasn't a road all the way through Labrador.

The key to my research turned up when I learned the Trans-Labrador Highway between Labrador City in the west and Goose Bay on Hamilton Inlet on the Atlantic coast was scheduled for completion that summer. We wouldn't find a four-lane highway lined with glittering service centres and Burger Kings, but the road would be the final link of a new access to the island of Newfoundland.

"Maybe I could be one of the first to tow a travel trailer across that new road," I thought to myself.

We would live in luxury throughout the trip in an eight-metre Airstream travel trailer.

I enticed Ron King and Toronto photographer John Stephens to join me on different stages of the 3000-kilometre labyrinth of roads and ferry boats we would encounter. We would live in luxury throughout the trip in an eight-metre Airstream travel trailer.

On a cool July morning, Ron King and I did a final equipment check. He had flown up from Tennessee the day before, and appreciated the clear fresh Maritime air. I showed Ron how to operate the Jimmy's 3600-kilogram winch that had been installed for a previous trip to Iceland. We adjusted all four auxiliary lights. The streamlined tandem-axle Airstream was packed with food and drink, tools, lots of fly dope and a thousand assorted bits and pieces. We hitched it to the Jimmy with a series of hoses, wires, cantilevers, and some other parts with the words EA-Z-Lift emblazoned on their sides that looked like they had fallen off a UFO.

The sky was much clearer than the week before when it had been filled with a murky haze that smelled faintly of smoke, giving the sun an unusual orange tint. Forest fires had been raging near Baie Comeau, north of the St. Lawrence River where we were headed and had blown smoke and ash nearly 700 kilometres south.

Hopefully the clear air meant the fires had been put out. We pulled away fully aware that if they were not extinguished before we hit the St. Lawrence, we would have to use the only alternative available to get the truck and trailer to Labrador City - a flatcar on a freight train from Sept Isles, Quebec.

Sunburned, fly-bitten, and stress-free... John Stephens (left), Ron King (right) and I had achieved the desired effect.

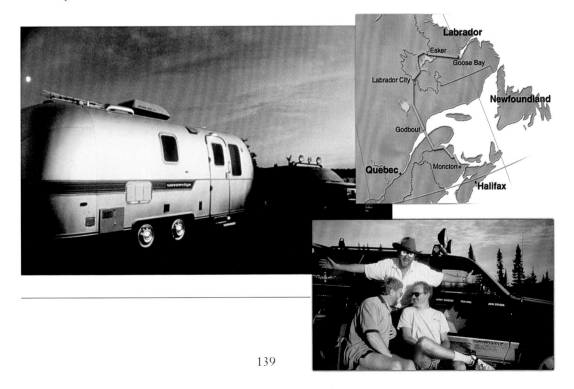

139

Along with the fires, another problem was surfacing in Goose Bay. We heard a bridge on the new road connecting Labrador City to Goose Bay was probably not completed. There was no way to be sure until we got there.

At the end of the first day we arrived in Matane, a French-Canadian town on the south bank of the St. Lawrence. There was a smoky haze in the air. We caught the next boat to Godbout, on the north shore where local police warned the danger of fire still existed. We would have to join a vehicle caravan in the morning to drive Route 389 through the fire zones.

I had a lousy night's sleep.

In the morning, we positioned ourselves behind a dozen cars and trucks, some with canoes strapped to their tops. Others were towing tent trailers. Quebec Provincial Police, in immaculate tan and blue uniforms, were registering vehicles for the convoy. Helicopters were coming and going from the landing pad beside our staging area through an atmosphere thick with dirty gray ash. A roadside sign in French said something about 'Manic 5' with an arrow pointing up the road. I wondered what it meant.

"Rough going ahead with lots of hills, a few possible flare-ups and lingering smoke," advised Ron, climbing into our grimy truck. Soot and cinders were collecting on everything. "The police say we should clear the fires in three or four hours."

During a final hitch check, I eyed the propane tanks which had just

Rule #134d: Keep an eye on cheery rail workers when they strap your trailer to a freight train.

been filled by a gas station attendant to a level that made me feel uncomfortable. A mud-splattered white Cadillac towing a U-Haul trailer was the last vehicle in line, and we were right in front of it. An hour and a half later, it would blow by us while we wrestled the renegade propane hose.

The episode with the hose left us too far behind the convoy to try and safely catch up. Fortunately the smoke cleared within a couple of hours, and we spent the next two days settling into the drive and admiring the scenery. We ate dust on some rather miserable stretches of road, then sailed over sections of smooth blacktop. We saw Manic 5 and realized it was not a camp for exiled maniacs, but part of one of the largest hydroelectric projects in the world. Running Route 389 was like playing connect-the-dots on a series of roads between deserted mining camps.

John Stephens wrestles the errant pork chops for kitchen domination.

****

The weather was hot and dry when we got to Labrador City, a tidy mining town near the Quebec border. We registered at Duley Lake Provincial Park's campground just west of town, where the local Ranger warned we might have to evacuate because a forest fire burned 20 kilometres away, and was moving closer. We set up camp and watched water bombers skim their loads from the lake beside us, then vanish into the dusk between the flames on the horizon and us.

"Enough of these fires," I said to Ron, who was devouring some of the fettuccine Alfredo he had casually whipped up. "Tomorrow we'll pick John up at the airport. I wonder if the road to Goose Bay is finished yet."

John Stephens' airplane arrived from Toronto, and the three of us swapped stories over a couple of Black Horse beers back at the lake that night. The following morning, John and I dropped the sunburned, fly-bitten Tennessee journalist off at the airport on our way to Goose Bay.

****

The road from Labrador City to Goose Bay was complete, with the exception of a 20-metre section of bridge over the narrows of Ossokmanuan

Lake, not far from the site of a massive hydroelectric project at Churchill Falls. Our only option across the narrows was a construction barge, which was one metre too short for the trailer, so we had to backtrack over 160 kilometres of loose gravel to Labrador City and wait for the train. The place we couldn't get to at first became the place we couldn't leave.

The thirty-car train bound for Schefferville, Quebec carried freight and an assortment of automobiles, trucks, and schoolhouses. Four passenger coaches were connected directly behind the trio of diesel electric locomotives. Cheerful workman chained the Jimmy and trailer to a flatcar near the end of the train. Then John and I stowed away inside the Airstream for the ride to Esker, where an industrial access road would lead us to Churchill Falls.

We had a couple of beers and entertained ourselves watching a food party unfold after we accidentally left the fridge and cupboard doors unlocked. During the seven-hour ride through absolute desolation, the refrigerator contents finally got to meet the pantry stuff. The cleaning supplies cornered the pork chops that had escaped from the freezer. The cooking oil went on a rampage, smashing three plastic glasses before dumping itself on a wandering roll of toilet paper. The lettuce rolled into the bathroom accompanied by a can of artichoke hearts.

We laughed, hysterically at times, as the trailer heaved back and forth on the flatcar.

After unloading in Esker we departed for Churchill Falls, 110 kilometres

Before we set off, some of the neighborhood kids including daughters Lucy (far left) and Natalie (far right) tried to get in on the action.

away. With the sun setting behind us, we were alone on a narrow dirt track in the middle of nowhere.

"The brakes feel a little funny," I told John, as I maneuvered down the dusty trail. It wasn't until I crawled under the trailer in the morning that I could see the severed wires to all four electric brakes. New Rule #134d in my books... Always keep an eye on where cheery rail workers attach the chains when they strap your trailer to a freight train.

"Hope there's no steep hills ahead," laughed John, smearing more fly dope on his neck.

But there were plenty of hills, and we hauled our silver albatross up and down 12% grades. It was the worst road of the trip, and we took 12 hours to cover the 320 kilometres to Goose Bay. There was no time to fish for dinner, so John fried up a pan of frozen fish sticks while I tried to repair the trailer brakes.

"There are three different kinds of falsehoods here," I joked to John, scratching my way through our pathetic meal. "Mosquitoes drill holes in your arms and neck while blackflies remove little hunks of skin. The resulting crater swells into a tiny maroon pimple. I haven't had a fight with one of those horseflies yet…"

We had created the desired effect: no telephone calls, no hassles, no getting sent to the store.

Vacation à la Labrador.

34. *Far-Off Dentist*

I get excited when Jane Tingley from my dentist's office calls to announce it's time for a check-up. Even if she wants to schedule work on a pesky root canal I still get a lift because my dentist is in another city of another province, almost three hundred kilometres away.

Yes, the need to see Dr. Rick Cole in Moncton, New Brunswick requires me to hit the road from Halifax for a quick visit to my hometown. Dentist Day is a chance to pick my route, select my music and sometimes even choose what to drive. It's an opportunity to see what's new on the main drag and check out old eating haunts. Sometimes I catch up on gossip with a crony or even spot a lady I had a high school crush on.

A call to tooth involves writing off a full day because a 600-kilometre road trip is part of the deal.

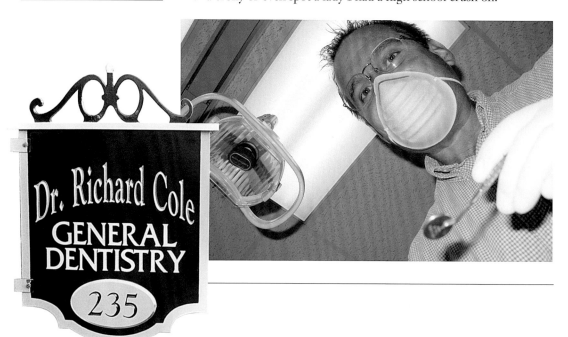

As a kid, the dentist meant missing an hour or two of school. As long as they weren't yanking out teeth, dental appointments in those pre-fluoride treatment days were a break from routine for the inconvenience of a cavity or two. Frozen lips guaranteed laughs back at school.

Business can wait. Responsibilities get shuffled. My kids and Lisa know I'll be out of the loop for the day. The night before the appointment, I fall asleep excited rather than anxious.

When friends ask why I have a dentist 300 kilometres away, I tell them it's because I'm lucky enough to be able to write off Dentist Day. With a home office, winter storms never grant a surprise day off so Dentist Day is my snow day, without the driveway to shovel. A trip to see Dr. Cole and Terry, his wife and hygienist, is a work break, hometown reunion, road trip and 'stress flush' all in one.

I recently got the call for a check-up and cleaning the very day I was rummaging for an excuse to put a new Saab 9-3 sport sedan I had borrowed through its paces. Dentist Day would also augment a pampering routine I was laying on myself since Lisa announced my hands were so dry they looked like they belonged on something out of a 1950s sci-fi flick.

Before my early morning departure, I selected music CDs that would draw long looks from my kids, packed a map so I could try the Saab on some twisty Nova Scotia back roads and kissed off responsibility for the day. I was going to the dentist and the world would be just fine until I plugged in again.

I took the direct route to Moncton while listening to a Time Life collection of folk music I had ordered from a late night infomercial. While Arlo Guthrie and the Rooftop Singers reminded me of how simple music once was, I admired my supple-looking hands on the steering wheel. Since Lisa had given me the word on geezer hands, I had been faithfully moisturizing them with hand lotion from a cache of small hotel-room bottles that find their way into my luggage.

The relaxed state in which I arrived at Dr. Cole's office was stoked from the minute I walked in.

"How's your mother?" Jane Tingley asked. She used to live near my parents and always wanted the latest news.

After settling into the hygienist's chair, Terry Cole entertained me with

Who else gets to see all this stuff on the way to their dentist? A 50s-era mascot for the commercial truck driving school in Debert, Nova Scotia; An intriguing mural in Amherst, NS and historic Fort Beauséjour at the head of the Bay of Fundy.

the antics of a recent Caribbean cruise she and Rick had taken with their 3 young children. Details about the idyllic week got me through the ordeal of scraping and polishing, feeling more like I was at a health spa, not in a dental chair with someone digging at my teeth.

Just before Dr. Cole checked me over, Terry announced that she and Rick had recently run the Amsterdam Marathon. As the dentist hovered over me with his tools, he seemed like someone completely different than the guy who knows my mouth better than I do. Realizing he could run 42 kilometres made it feel like a demi-god was caring for my teeth.

Dr. Cole sent me off with a good report. I cruised Main Street but didn't see any familiar faces so I left for Halifax stopping a half-hour later in Sackville, New Brunswick where I had attended Mount Allison University. I washed the Saab at the coin wash and checked out the campus. Then I ventured into the Bridge Street Café for a cappuccino. Across the street the Vogue Theatre looked the same as when I walked by it on my way to classes in 1972.

After crossing into Nova Scotia, I worked the Saab over a series of back roads skirting the head of the Bay of Fundy. As I played the 5-speed gearbox, the response of the silky turbocharged engine added to my feelings of contentment. I was having a self-indulging day, my dental team

The Saab 9-3 was the perfect accomplice for a Dentist Day escapade.

were marathon runners and the hometown was still in one piece. The coffee break in Sackville brought me back to carefree college days.

I decided to stop for an ice cream. Why not? Nobody would know. Get them to plop two big scoops of butterscotch ripple on top and have my way with that cone. It's Dentist Day and I got off with a clean slate.

I picked up a loaf of fresh homemade bread, a guilt pacifier. It would let everyone at home know that, even on Dentist Day, I'm still thinking of them.

As I finished off the ice cream, the cell phone rang. It was Lisa.

"I have a present for you," I offered, eyeing the golden loaf of bread on the passenger's seat.

"I'm sitting at your desk," she stated, in an I've-got-something-on-you voice.

My mind raced trying to determine what she could have unearthed. Her lost pens? The postage stamps I sneak from her stash?

"I've got your moisturizer here." I figured she was going to razz me about forgetting the hand cream in my haste to get started on Dentist Day.

"Oh well, I guess in the rush to break free, eerrr, get going, I must have forgotten it." I admired my silky hands on the steering wheel.

"Hair conditioner," she said dryly.

Look, Ma! No cavities! Dr. Rick Cole validates another road trip.

147

35. Saskatchewan Dreamin'

The menu at the Dunn Inn was nothing fancy, just a single laminated page featuring basic fare: chicken strips, club sandwich, some predictable entrées and a slew of hot sandwiches. The top third of the page was devoted to breakfast, the middle to the sandwiches and the bottom to something I hadn't seen for a long time… supper suggestions.

It reminded me of my youth in Moncton, New Brunswick where the noon meal was dinner and the evening meal was supper. Lunch was something you lugged to school in a brown paper bag or wolfed down before going to bed. But in tiny Consul, tucked between two ghost towns in the southwest corner of Saskatchewan, supper seemed a proper thing to call the evening meal.

Lisa went for pork chops with all the fixin's and I ordered pork cutlets from the cheerful bright-eyed waitress who was hustling around the tidy restaurant preparing a birthday party for one of the 92 inhabitants of Consul. With 14 party-goers on hand, I figured about 18% of Consul's population was in there, checking out the supper suggestions and the two strangers in the corner.

In due course, we were approached by Warren Seifert, a bear of a man with an infectious grin. He wanted to know if we were driving the Escalade EXT angle-parked out front with the Ontario license plates. It was not the first time on our trip through the back roads of Saskatchewan that the techie, black pick-up version of Cadillac's SUV had been a catalyst for conversation. Warren went into a surprising degree of detail about the EXT; all-wheel drive, 345 horsepower, its reconfiguration features. His son has just ordered one and Warren had obviously done his homework.

It turned out that he and his wife, Linda, have a fair stake in Consul. They manage the Dunn Inn, own the ten-unit motel next door and she cooks at the restaurant. He teaches at the regional high school, runs a woodworking shop and drives the school bus 290 kilometres a day. Warren's spare time is spent fussing over a mint 1978 Caddy Eldorado that his father bequeathed to him.

Driving through Saskatchewan should always include a healthy dose of backroads and prairie towns.

Within minutes, it felt more like we were visiting a favorite aunt and uncle than sitting in a place I had never heard of until we rolled in with a bad case of the road munchies.

But that's how Lisa and I felt time and time again during our four-day junket across the province. I've had a soft spot for Saskatchewan since taking two jet training programs at Moose Jaw with the Canadian military in the early '70s. People out there look you straight in the eye when they talk to you. They ask direct questions. They want to know what you think about their part of the world, still talk distance in miles and are guaranteed to ask what the weather is like where you live. They remind me of New Brunswickers, who also live in a place most travellers drive through on their way to somewhere else, missing a lot in the process.

Our trek through Saskatchewan was part of a 4-week drive from Halifax to Vancouver planning a drive program for an upcoming automotive product launch. It gave us a chance to put the snazzy Escalade EXT through its paces. The muffled growl of its 6-litre V-8 brought me back to some of those muscle cars I used to test drive in Regina on my days off from flight school 30 years earlier.

Those hopelessly straight backroads with absolutely no traffic provided lots of temptation to find out what all those horsepower could do until Lisa pointed out the onboard computer that could track the vehicle's total distance for each of the past 15 days. It also displayed the maximum speed for those days. Needless to say, the highest top speed of our trip occurred the day before we made this discovery.

With a travel schedule that called for us to change hotels every night, I soon found myself travelling just as much in my sleep as on our daily transits. One night, after cruising the back trails up in the Cypress Hills, I dreamed I followed a remote logging trail high into the sky to an exclusive paradise plateau where, for some reason, I had to stay hidden while watching smiling Sackatchewans fishing and picnicking in a summer utopia. The dream went on forever as I watched them gleefully hauling limitless salmon out of a turquoise swimming pool.

Warren Seifert looks over our Escalade in front of a mural depicting his father's service station and Warren himself on his first set of wheels.

The following day we drove out to the ice fishing huts on frozen Round Lake in pretty Qu'Appelle Valley. That night, more dreams put a six-pound salmon in my briefcase that I kept carrying back to meetings in Toronto. I couldn't get rid of that fish no matter how many times I woke up. In one of those weird only-in-a-dream ways, the salmon became my business card. What would the Tele-psychics make of that?

The night we spent in Consul, I tossed and turned as I became a close confident to Russia's President Vladimir Putin who had moved to Saskatchewan and had caught their contagious friendliness. He loved a place where people celebrated a day for mothers. The fact that the provincial government was in the vehicle insurance business thrilled him, too.

The next morning, Linda cooked Lisa and I breakfast at the Dunn Inn. Warren dropped by in the school bus. After a warm farewell, we climbed into the Escalade and headed west toward the Alberta border. A half dozen deer stood by the road at the edge of Consul and watched as we slipped through the icy morning fog.

I figured I had seen the last of President Putin. There was no salmon in my briefcase, just a map of Alberta and a list of meetings in Lethbridge, Calgary and Banff.

And when the fog lifted, there would be cowboys, oil rigs and those distant Rocky Mountains waiting to welcome us.

But supper would be dinner that night. I was pretty sure of that.

Saskatchewan landmarks: big sky, hopelessly straight roads and the ever-present grain trains.

36. Humpbacks, Bergy Bits and Toutons

Grates Cove, Newfoundland, on the northernmost point of the Avalon peninsula.

The spartan rooms at The Captain's Inn were spotless with pastel blue walls that would have looked more at home across the road at the Old Perlican Hospital. Lisa and I unpacked and headed downstairs to the restaurant where the innkeeper, Carol Strong, was fussing over our dinner of fried cod tongues, boiled potatoes and sweet corn.

During dinner she hovered over the table filling our heads with the gossip and lore of Old Perlican, whose harbour has been in use since 1570. I asked how we could be eating cod tongues when fishing cod was illegal.

"The Russians, dear. They fish 'em beyond the limits and sell 'em back to us." She had an answer to any question we threw at her.

After dinner, Carol asked if we planned on going out. Since the wind was howling enough to rattle the windows, I was noncommital.

"Aw, yer the only ones here tonight so I'm goin' home. Help yer selves to the bar and anything else you need. I'll be back 'bout nine tomorrow morning," she said, tossing me the keys to the hotel.

Another first. After thirty-five years of travelling the planet I have never had an innkeeper throw me the keys to their establishment so they could go home for the night. But this was Newfoundland.

We had arrived in Newfoundland the day before by ferry boat from Nova Scotia to Port Aux Basques on the Island's west coast. Then we drove 900 kilometres across the province to St John's with one goal in mind… find the best one-day drive loop out of North America's oldest city. That limited us to the Avalon Peninsula, a windswept jut of rock hanging off the southeast corner of Canada's most easterly province.

After some map work, we decided to go for the Baccalieu Trail, a 400-kilometre drive around the perimeter of the Avalon's northern finger that separates Trinity and Conception Bays.

The first 90 kilometres out of St. John's took us west along the Trans Canada Highway. A good stretch to relax and enjoy the rolling countryside dotted with small pristine lakes the locals call ponds and erratics, huge boulders dropped by age-old glaciers creeping south. It also gave us a chance to figure out what to expect at our first stop, a place called Dildo where we met Gerald Smith, a fisherman who had started a whale-watching business after a moratorium on cod fishing was imposed in 1992.

Over the years, the quaint fishing community has processed cod, herring, whales, seals and squid. They were even into mink ranching of all things. Gerald took us into the Dildo Interpretation Centre, a place I figured might offer an explanation for the village's name, and showed us a replica of the monstrous 6-metre squid found washed up on the Dildo beach in 1933. Although Dildonians are very proud of the name of their village, aside from a string of smirks and innuendoes, we never did find out how the name originated.

In a rich Newfoundland accent, Gerald explained how Dildo Harbour was a great place to spot whales. Sure enough, as we chatted

Aside from a string of smirks and innuendos, we never did find out how the village of Dildo got its name.

Our GMC Sierra was the first of the redesigned pickups on the road in Newfoundland.

and munched on grilled caplins, a humpback surfaced a few hundred metres off the wharf where a prominent sign warned 'No Cleaning of Seals or Fish on Docks'.

North of Dildo, the two-lane paved road wound along the coast through the likes of Heart's Delight and Heart's Desire to Heart's Content where the first transatlantic communication cable was laid. The road continued north through remote fishing villages with rustic wharves, weathered fish-processing sheds and unassuming saltbox houses.

Then we saw it, towering 10 storeys out of the water. It had run aground in Sibley's Cove where the afternoon sun turned the massive hunk of Greenland ice a fluorescent bluish-white color. It looked more like something from another planet than our preconceived ideas of what an iceberg should look like. At a weight in the 100-million-ton range, it wasn't going far. Further north, most of the coves had their own gigantic visitors, huge air conditioners powered by the summer winds.

So, four hours after leaving St. John's, we pulled into Old Perlican and checked into The Captain's Inn. After filling up on cod tongues and Carol's neighborhood news, we took an evening stroll through Old Perlican past a fish-processing plant that is one of the most successful in all of Newfoundland. The moratorium on cod fishing forced the area's fishermen to concentrate on snow crab resulting in staggering yields which are sold to Japanese businessmen for tables halfway around the world.

In the morning, we stopped for fuel at a station down the road from The Captain's Inn. The local policeman bombarded us with questions about the newly restyled GMC Sierra truck we were driving. Since it was the very first one on the road in Newfoundland, it became the centre of attention everywhere we stopped. Just what we needed, an icebreaker in the land of the friendliest people in the world. Five minutes later Mr. Policeman is treating Lisa to a coffee while I am out in the parking lot playing with the squad car.

The officer suggested we take the coast route up to Grates Cove, the next stop on our trek. The 15-kilometre dirt road presented more icebergs, some surrounded by growlers and bergy bits, small bergs that had broken off from the 'mothership'.

The village of Grates Cove sits at the northernmost point of the

peninsula where the trees give way to stunted shrubbery and bald rock faces. Legend has it that John Cabot first landed here and left an inscription on a rock supposedly stolen by some 'media people' in the 1960s. With almost as many graveyards and churches as houses, Grates Cove made us feel like we were at the end of the Earth. Off the coast a few kilometres, loom the red cliffs of Baccalieu Island, home to thousands of sea birds going about their business. In my mind's eye, I could see Cabot's ship out there bobbing around in the steel blue swell.

From Grates Cove, the trail heads south along the coast of Conception Bay. Every turn held a surprise. Grounded icebergs shimmering in the dazzling sunshine. One looked like the *U.S.S. Enterprise*. A whale off in the distance breaching. We cruised through Burnt Point, Gull Island and Blackhead… outlying communities set in a wonderland of water, rock and ice.

The road continued north through remote fishing villages with rustic wharves, weathered fish-processing sheds and unassuming saltbox houses.

At Salmon Cove, we diverted onto a single-lane track that brought us in the back door of Carbonear, the commercial centre of the Baccalieu Trail. The community is saturated with folklore ranging from Irish princesses to seal hunts gone bad. After a good soaking, we continued south to Harbour Grace where Peter Easton, an infamous privateer turned pirate, battled the Spanish invaders.

However, we were more interested in setting foot on the Harbour Grace airfield on top of a hill overlooking the town. The grass strip was built in 1927 as a launch point for most of the first transatlantic flights as well as a fuelling stop for early around-the-world attempts. This is where Amelia Earhart took off on her perilous 15-hour flight to Londonderry, Northern Ireland, securing her spot in the history books as the first woman to fly solo across the Atlantic Ocean.

At the strip we encountered Mr. Gordon Pike, head of the Harbour Grace Historical Society. How convenient, a living encyclopaedia crammed with stories about the town that at one time was competing with St John's for capital city status. Later he took us to the Gordon Pike Railway Museum for tea and toutons, a local concoction of fried bread dough smothered in molasses.

South of Harbour Grace, we passed the *S.S. Kyle*, a silent sentinel to the history of the area. She was used as a ferry for fishermen, a sealing vessel, then as a rescue ship for airplanes that went down after taking off from the airstrip. Unfortunately she ran aground 30 years ago, drifting south after breaking from her moorings up the coast at the Carbonear wharf. She's been listing in Harbour Grace harbour ever since.

We drove south through Spaniard's Bay, Black Duck Pond and Cupids, the first English settlement in North America. Then inland over the

barrens to the Trans Canada Highway and back to St John's. We checked into the luxurious Hotel Newfoundland with its panoramic view of the city and harbour. The room was posh with an array of complimentary nuts and candies.

We swam in the indoor pool then relaxed in the hot tub. That night at the hotel's renowned restaurant we feasted on culinary delights prepared by a world-class chef. Everyone was amiable. The food was fabulous. The service impeccable.

But no one offered us the keys to the joint and said they'd be back in the morning.

That, we figured, was a ritual reserved for The Captain's Inn back on the Baccalieu Trail.

In June and July, the Baccalieu Trail offers prime viewing points from which to behold the annual parade of icebergs.

37. Back Roads and Avalanche Loads

"They roam around here till they die of old age." Mark sounded like he was talking about family.

The 24 fence posts had to be exactly 2.46 metres long. The rolled wire fencing could be no higher than 161 cm. Sacks of feed were a good bet. The 4-grain scratch, hog mash and rolled oats all came in 40-kilo bags which could be handled by one person. The 2-metre long galvanized water trough was not cheap at $179.95 but it would do the trick. We'd pick up the ice and groceries later.

Salt licks? I had never actually laid my hands on one before, but the 20-kilo pale blue blocks seemed like a deal at $7.95 each. I piled five onto the pallet so the forklift could transfer them onto the back of the truck we had rented to haul the 'loads' to the staging area in Oshawa, Ontario.

Then the real work got underway as we tried to figure out a way to

pack these items into nine shiny new Chevy Avalanche trucks. Normally this would be easy, but this was not your run-of-the-mill pickup truck. By reconfiguring its Midgate system through a series of easy-to-use latches, the 4-door truck's cargo box quickly extends inward almost an extra metre providing load flexibility, security and weather resistance.

The loads were to be an important component during a 5-hour demonstration intended to give motoring media a chance to experience the quirky new Avalanche. The loads would give them a hands-on feel for Avalanche's adaptability from a 5-passenger people-mover to a cargo hauler with almost as many configurations as a 'Kitchen Magician'.

Developing the route was straightforward. Lisa and I drove a few thousand kilometres over a slew of backroads between Oshawa and Muskoka in cottage country north of Toronto. We came up with a variety of freeway, secondary and gravel roads while dodging a zoo of wildlife that the humid early summer heat had mobilized.

A few months earlier during a similar event for American journalists in Palm Springs, we worked with Apple Canyon Centre, a camp that actor Dustin Hoffman helped establish to give children with cancer free camping experiences. And, since we figured those journalists would enjoy trying out Avalanches with real loads rather than something that made no sense, we convinced the folks at Chevrolet to let us purchase items the camp really needed. So the Avalanches got a real job and the woodsplitter, generator, compressor washer, dryer and other useful equipment were greatly appreciated at the camp.

In Canada, we came across Quaker Oaks Farm near Sebright on Highway 45 where owners Mark and Judy Spurr run an operation that includes a sanctuary for abandoned and abused farm animals. Lisa and I were first drawn to their quaint yellow curio shop where we snapped up very funky presents for our kids and my mother-in-law.

"What do you do with all the animals?" Lisa asked Mark, as he packaged a metallic toy duck with a propeller on its head.

"They roam around here till they die of old age." Mark sounded like he was talking about family. "There's Meryl Sheep, Gloria the pig, goats Penelope and Baby, and some fine-feathered fowl that follow each other around till they get dizzy."

We liked this place and we liked Judy and Mark, so we told them about

Top: *Paul Solomons, Derrick Bemister (in truck), and Bill Rumsey transferring the loads.*

Middle: *Martha the pig*

Bottom: *Lisa finds fellowship with Gloria*

Mark Spurr making time with Betty Boop

Below: *Quaker Oaks Farm near Sebright, Ontario*

our drive program and offered to bring nine Avalanches stuffed with items to help care for the critters if they would cater a lunch for 25 journalists and General Motors executives.

There was a catch though. The food had to be as good as the baguette sandwiches, garlic-stuffed olives and cherry pepper bombs we had just devoured at their store. They looked at us as if we had just crawled out of a flying saucer, flashed smiles which we would become used to seeing, and agreed.

Drive day came and our crew did a fine job flipping Midgates, packing fence posts and placing salt licks on PRO-TEC tailgates. They separated bagged insulation from the groceries with load dividers and poured ice inside Top-Box Storage compartments to keep pop and juice cold all day. Some Avalanches had the rear glass in, some out. Cargo covers on some, off on others. Weather-sensitive and valuable loads were covered and secure.

The lunch spread Mark and Judy laid out would rival that of the trendiest of hot spots. The buffet feast of tabouleh salad, hardy minestrone soup, overstuffed sandwiches and Judy's out-of-this-world butter tarts was down-home and unpretentious.

In the end, the journalists seemed to have had a good time, the trucks ran well and Mark and Judy appreciated the loads. But the biggest show of gratitude came when Mark opened the barn doors after everyone had left.

Out burst a parade of geese, turkeys, guinea fowl and goats. They obviously weren't used to being herded into the barn while trucks and journalists stomped around their barnyard. In the bright sunlight, their squinting eyes reminded me of those Saturday afternoons coming out of a matinee theatre as a kid.

Once outside they all stopped short and stared at the pile of salt licks, fence posts, fencing and feed. Squawks, chirps and bleats filled the air as they shuffled around the booty.

As we pulled out of the driveway, I noticed two geese and a rooster tearing at the side of a bag of 4-grain scratch.

Bok!

Left to right: *Sarah, Mark, Aden, Jillian, Tristan and Judy Spurr in their curio shop at Quaker Oaks Farm.*

Chapter 6 *Three Parts Horn, One Part Driving*

*W*hen one of the sentries at the French Foreign Legion Post saluted, I snapped one back. 'Men Who Would be Kings' all right, at least till we got off the train in this place I couldn't even pronounce.

38. The Red Sea Smuggler

I awoke at 5:20 that April morning on a flatcar at the end of a creeping freight train. My partner Ken Langley and our Ethiopian guide, Tim Cat, were asleep wrapped in grubby horsehair blankets to fend off the chilly desert dawn.

Below the trestle we were clanging over, a woman chased a child as he threw stones at her. At the end of the trestle, I noticed a decomposing camel carcass, another victim of the trains making their way to the exotic port of Djibouti, strategically situated at the mouth of the Red Sea between Ethiopia and Somalia.

Although groggy, it didn't take long to remember it was Day 9 of our attempt to set a new world driving record between Cape Agulhas, at the southern tip of Africa, and Nord Cape high above the Arctic Circle in Norway. Our specially-equipped six-month-old 1984 GMC Suburban, sporting nine bullet holes from an ambush in Kenya a few days earlier, was chained to the flatcar as it carried us over the last 200 kilometres of the African sector of the adventure. On the roof of the boxcars up front,

Our bullet-riddled GMC Suburban was chained to a flatcar for the last 200 kilometres of the African sector of our adventure.

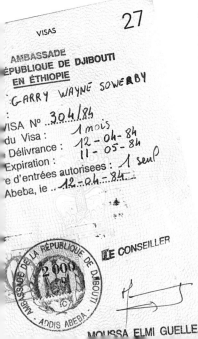

Crowds bid farewell as we departed Dire Dawa, Ethiopia en route to the Republic of Djibouti.

twenty well-equipped soldiers, bent on delivering us safely out of Ethiopian territory, diligently eyed the desolate countryside.

At the Djibouti border Tim Cat bid us a warm farewell, probably happy to see the end of us. Pulling into the dusty, fortified city I felt a deep sense of accomplishment because, no matter what happened from then on, we had made it through Africa. When one of the sentries at the French Foreign Legion Post saluted, I snapped one back. 'Men Who Would be Kings' all right, at least till we got off the train in this place I couldn't even pronounce.

We off-loaded the truck and secured it in the customs compound. Exhausted, we checked into a modest hotel on the shore of the Red Sea with an air conditioner that sounded like the radial engines on a DC-3 aircraft.

After cleaning up I called our only contact in Djibouti, the Roman Catholic Bishop who, through a contact, had promised to help with arrangements to get the Suburban and us across the Red Sea to Saudi Arabia.

He wanted to meet us at eight that evening at a downtown saloon so we took a nap, woke up freezing in that pit of a room, and headed for the rendezvous. The cavernous bar, packed with soldiers and seamen, reminded me of a scene from a James Bond movie.

The Bishop arrived right on time. After sharing a few beverages, the hip-looking, middle-aged cleric 'fessed up to having problems finding a guaranteed way of getting us and the truck across the Red Sea.

"I spoke to the Father last night," he said with a grin. "And although he did it for Moses a few thousand years ago, he wouldn't do it for a couple of Nova Scotians. But I have the next best thing."

He went on to tell us of an acqaintance who would transport the truck across the Red Sea to Jizan, a super-tanker port in southern Saudi Arabia, for $5,000. He would use a 40-foot wooden Arab dhow sailboat but, because of the threat of piracy, we would not be allowed to travel with the truck. Ken and I would have to fly ahead to Saudi and wait, rendering the truck out of our control on the high seas for five days. The plan sounded edgy but, since it was the only game in town, we had to agree.

The next day we made arrangements for the cash, picked up the Bishop and drove to the port. The heat was beyond ridiculous as we were introduced to the Bishop's contact. He had a large gold earring, a slippery look about him and wore a skirt. His crew of three looked like 12-year-old boys sporting sparse mustaches.

A crane lowered the loaded truck onto the boat's deck crossways with the bumpers hanging over the siderails. The rickety sailboat sank another metre into the water affirming the precariousness of the situation.

I pulled the Bishop aside. "Look, he has our truck, all our equipment, our $5,000 and we don't even have any insurance on that unregistered tub."

"Yes, but he has a family I know here in Djibouti as well as a reputation as an honest operator. And he charged you a hefty fee. If it had been $500, I'd be worried. He'll deliver." The Bishop was persuasive.

Just before they shoved off, I remembered the gold Krugerrand my father-in-law had given me before leaving Halifax, advising there may be a time when I would need gold to get out of a jam. I fished it out of my wallet and flashed it at Mr. Skirt. It was an ounce of solid gold and he knew it. I asked the Bishop to tell him it would be a tip for safely delivering the truck to Jizan.

Ken Langley (right) and I arranging money transfers in Djibouti.

I had an ache in the pit of my stomach watching the small, frail boat disappear into the humid haze. I thought we would never see the truck again and return to Canada looking like fools to have invested in the dubious operation.

Five days later, Ken and I met with the head of the port authority in Jizan, Saudi Arabia. A letter from a Saudi Prince that a GM executive had obtained for us was working wonders in terms of expediency and respect.

Surprisingly, we were advised the boat had arrived the night before and was tied up at pier 12. We were given a ride over and, sure enough, way down below the pier between two huge super-tankers was the Suburban looking like a toy on a toy boat. The crew cheered as a crane hoisted the truck and Mr. Skirt up onto the pier.

I pulled the Krugerrand out of my pocket and offered it to the man I had obviously judged incorrectly. He smiled and said something in Arabic.

"What did he say?" I asked the translator we had hired for the port meetings.

"He said, 'Keep it. You might need it in Iraq or somewhere else up the line.' "

The Bishop was right.

39. The Great Ascent

The technicians cheered as astonished tourists looked on in disbelief.

It was September 1989. I was on the telephone, talking to Rob Hutchison, about his new job in Toronto as the Central Region Special Events Manager for General Motors of Canada.

"We get a stack of requests to sponsor events every week. It's tough to decide which ones to support because there are so many to choose from. Some are pretty far out."

He went into detail about one such request to put a car into the observation deck near the top of Toronto's CN Tower. A year earlier, two men had carried a fridge and stove up the Tower's 1,760-step inner stairwell to draw attention to the pending United Way Stair Climb. The fundraiser relied on the public's ability to entice neighbours, uncles and the corner store owner to pledge so many dollars a step for climbing the Tower.

The proposal asked if GM could drive a car up the stairs of the Toronto landmark as a hype-builder for that year's Stair Climb, which was just three weeks away. Rob and I had a good laugh then went on to other topics.

That night I couldn't stop thinking about the CN Tower. I had driven from one side of it to the other nine years earlier when we used it as the start/finish point of our first around-the-world drive. The Tower's management had given me a lifetime pass to the observation deck at the end of that trip.

Before drifting off to sleep, I was convinced that, with three weeks of open calendar, I could figure out how to plan, finance and pull the necessary resources together to get a car up there.

The concept would be to set a tongue-in-cheek speed record from 'the bottom to the top of Toronto.' The bottom would be the lowest level of the underground parking lot of the Hotel Admiral which, at the time, was the closest to sea level you could drive to in Toronto. The top was one third of a kilometre above the city streets, on the observation deck of the CN Tower. The attempt would be called The Great Ascent.

The following week I visited the joint-venture GM/Suzuki CAMI car plant in Ingersoll, Ontario which was producing the first run of Pontiac Fireflys. I thought the sub-compact vehicle might be a candidate. I visited two other assembly plants. More engineers, more line workers and more bad news about finding a car that would do what we needed it to do.

It came down to two contenders: a Suzuki Samurai or an MG Midget. In both vehicles, the windshield posts on either side were removable, which was a critical component to our plan's success.

The final decision went to the Samurai. I presented the idea to the Public Relations department at Suzuki Canada Inc. and they climbed aboard. Excitement was building.

Over the next two weeks, sponsors were secured and a crew of more than 70 volunteers was recruited. The start location was surveyed and my navigator, a very capable-looking Pinkerton security guard, was briefed.

At the start, a briefcase, containing a $6,000-donation to the United Way, was handcuffed to the navigator's left wrist. We wound our way out of the parking garage and drove to the CN Tower, less than a kilometre away. At the base of the Tower, we were welcomed by a crew of nine

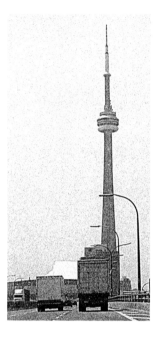

Rob Hutchison got the ball rolling for our storming of Toronto's CN Tower, the world's tallest free-standing structure.

The engine was another story for eight people who tortured themselves for an hour and thirty-two minutes.

technicians and an unlikely platoon of 44 'hard-bodies' from moving companies, fitness centres and cycling clubs.

It was the ultimate pit stop. Tools flew as the technicians stripped down the Samurai and handed the parts to the waiting platoon who, in turn, lugged them up the zig-zag stairway to the top of the world's tallest free-standing structure. I carried the steering wheel, a cellular phone and a walkie-talkie through the traffic jam of people, car parts and sweat. En route, I was passed by the exhaust system, the transmission and the rear differential, before running into gridlock behind the hood and the bulky rear body sections, about 200 stairs from the top.

The fastest part to reach the top was a tire and wheel assembly that made it in 20 minutes at a rate of 1.47 stairs per second. The engine was another story for eight people who tortured themselves for an hour and thirty-two minutes while a stockpile of parts grew on the observation deck. Since the first parts disassembled were generally the last parts to be assembled nothing could be done until the frame, which was near the end of the line, arrived.

When everything was at the top, the technicians put the Samurai back

together in just 59 minutes. I slipped behind the wheel, started the engine and drove a couple of metres across the finish line near the entrance of Sparkles Discotheque.

We had done it. From the bottom to the top of Toronto in five hours and 38 minutes at a blinding speed of .004367051 km/h. The technicians, sponsors and carriers cheered as astonished tourists looked on in disbelief. My navigator and I proudly presented the $6,000 to the United Way officials.

On the CTV National News that night, a story about The Great Ascent wrapped up the newscast. With Rimsky-Korsakov's *Flight of the Bumblebee* playing in the background, the disassembly, ascent and re-assembly of the Samurai were replayed at high speed. The news anchors chuckled through the sign-off.

A lot had gone on in the three weeks since Rob Hutchison gave me some insight into his stacks of proposals. All those people. The parts. The stairs. That's when I realized that, sometime in the next few months, someone would be getting another proposal.

It would be time to get the car off the top of the CN Tower.

Above: The tools were flying at the ultimate pit stop.

Below: Technicians, carriers and our sponsors celebrate The Great Ascent.

171

40. Long Night with an Eight-armed Goddess

"What kind of weapons are you carrying?"

It was the question I did not want to hear. And the matter-of-fact way in which Ahmad Homayouni asked it made me feel even worse. His relatives, gathered around the table at his cousin's home in Kerman, Iran, seemed to be staring right through me.

"Well, we don't have *any* weapons," I replied. I didn't like where this was headed.

Fifteen seconds. It seemed like an eternity. But for the next fifteen seconds, there was silence in this immense house with a garden in the living room. The half dozen Iranians stared at me as if I was crazy to be

Crossing Pakistan's Sandy Desert, known for its constant mirages and sudden severe sandstorms, en route from Zahedan, Iran to Quetta, Pakistan.

heading out unarmed on the desolate 600-kilometre road through Pakistan's Sandy Desert paralleling the Afghanistan border.

The ensuing conversation confirmed my suspicions about security in West Pakistan. Ahmad and his family explained that the area we were about to drive through was rife with smugglers moving three-cent-a-gallon Iranian gasoline into Pakistan. It was a region where tons of the world's opium and hashish start the journey to western markets and where gun runners arming Afghani rebels surface from time to time.

To make matters worse, they assured me the transportation of choice for many of these operatives was four-wheel drive sport utility vehicles. I eyed our grimy four-wheel drive Vauxhall Frontera turbo diesel out front in the driveway. The spare tires and satellite communications antennae on the roof made it look like a sitting duck.

In the fading desert light, I could just make out the logo on its front door, *Frontera World Challenge*. A muezzin chant from the mosque down the street filled the air. The heat was stifling. I was exhausted.

My partners, Welshman Colin Bryant and Scottish-born Graham McGaw, were down the street at the Kerman Grand Hotel. They were trying to overcome a technical glitch in our procedure for uploading digital images back to our logistics office in Canada and the press centre in London, England.

Meals on the road cost more than fuel in Iran where $1 bought 120 litres of diesel.

Colin, a retired police officer who spent much of his career driving British heads of state around Wales, was about the best driver I had ever been with in a car. Witty and charming, focused and stubborn, he had already wrestled our overloaded Frontera through many dicey traffic situations.

Graham knew every nut and bolt in our vehicle. He worked as an engineer at the plant where the Frontera, the European version of the Isuzu Rodeo, was manufactured in Luton, England. His natural curiosity, coupled with plenty of experience with everything from motorcycles to eighteen wheelers, made him ideal for the team.

Since leaving England, we had driven pretty well non-stop. Western Europe was straightforward. Aside from a two-hour traffic jam in Vienna and torrential downpours in Serbia, the 38-hour drive to Sofia, Bulgaria was a good warm-up. Then it was pea-soup fog through the mountains of central Turkey and temperatures of up to 42 Celsius in the desert areas southeast of Tehran.

The rules for the around-the-world driving record we were attempting stipulated that Colin, Graham and I had to drive at least 29,000 kilometres. Backtracking was not allowed and we had to finish with at least two of us in the car. The route had to pass through two antipodal points - places on the earth's sphere that are diametrically opposed to one another. Our antipodals were Gisborne, New Zealand and Sagunto, a town just outside of Valencia, Spain.

The clock ran during the continental transits only. Turn it on in London. Turn it off in Chennai, India. On in Perth, Australia. Off in Sydney and so on. So with five stages, the attempt became five record runs with breathers in between where we transformed ourselves into logisticians, documenteurs and administrators.

And finally the big ugly. No speeding. Get caught speeding and it's over in the eyes of Guinness Superlatives, who were sanctioning the attempt. There were a thousand things that could have ended the Challenge, but the idea of disqualification for a speeding ticket didn't excite any of us. And, since the only way to guarantee one didn't get a ticket was not to speed, we didn't. It wasn't that bad. It kept the stress levels down and we still managed to cover an amazing amount of territory every day.

All the way through the Sandy Desert, I thought about my three young daughters Lucy, Natalie and Layla back home in Nova Scotia. But in my mind's eye, I couldn't erase the visual of Graham's two children, Vikki, 7, and Andrew, 4, hugging their daddy goodbye at the start line. Their skinny outstretched arms reaching for one more embrace before we headed off. I envisioned that scene many times… when an ominous speck on the horizon grew into an approaching vehicle, when we detoured around blasted-out bridges…

Ahmad Homayouni's family wondered what weapons we would be carrying through Pakistan.

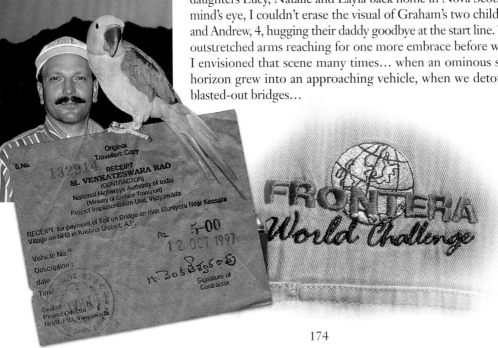

But, we made it through the desert without incident. It took three days to get through Pakistan to New Delhi, India. On the second day, the road was so rough it took 17 hours to cover just 600 kilometres. Then it was floods in Multan, bribes to get us out of Pakistan and an 11-hour night drive along India's Grand Trunk Road that would have made anyone's hair stand on end. We arrived in New Delhi at three in the morning, manoeuvring through a smoggy, ragged fog.

Our 2,300-kilometre route from New Delhi to Chennai (formerly Madras), on the Bay of Bengal in southeast India, was one tough drive. Colin woke up feeling sick in New Delhi and got progressively worse. South of Agra, home of the wondrous Taj Mahal, navigating got complicated. Most of the road signs were in the local script so we couldn't decipher

Colin Bryant's health was rapidly deteriorating as we departed India Gate, New Delhi's monument to fallen WWI soldiers.

Since Durga had the main roads blocked, we had to find alternate routing through back streets, back yards even.

the alphabet, let alone the words. It was tense. At one point, a crowd surrounded the car, some banging on the windows with their fists.

The road eventually deteriorated into one lane of pot-holed asphalt. Towns and villages were jammed with creeping trucks carrying huge *papier mâché* statues of the eight-armed goddess, Durga. Since Durga had the main roads blocked, we had to find alternate routing through back streets, back yards even. As we worked our way south, we saw people dumping her likenesses into lakes and rivers. It was a night I will never forget.

We drove all the next day and into the night along roads choked with chaotic traffic. A car once in a while but mostly trucks. Big grotesque ones. Some had one light, some had none. Few had all their lights. But one thing was certain, any truck with lights had the high beams staring right into our bloodshot eyes.

It had been 36 hours since we left New Delhi and Colin's condition had degenerated to a point where he was virtually helpless. It was very quiet in the backseat where he was laid out except for a guttural moan whenever Graham or I hit a pothole.

We finally reached Chennai 11 days, 21 hours and 25 minutes after leaving London… five minutes ahead of our self-imposed schedule. We were tired, filthy and Colin was a mess, but we were ecstatic to have reached the end of the first leg in our bid to drive around the world.

For the next two days, Graham checked over the Frontera, Colin recovered at the hotel and I dealt with the Indian bureaucracy. It was rubber-stamp madness as a shipping agent paraded me and a mountain of blurry documents around the port of Chennai. The place looked more like a landfill operation than a major international shipping centre. When word got around about where we had been, the Directors of both the Customs and Security departments got involved.

With our papers in order, I drove the Frontera into a well-used 6-metre container. A giant forklift loaded the container onto a flatbed truck for transport across the port to the ship. In three weeks, our truck would be in Perth, on Australia's west coast.

Black clouds had filled the sky while craggy forks of lightening danced along the horizon. The humidity was outrageous.

"You were lucky to get to Chennai when you did, Mister Garry," the Customs official warned.

"Why's that?" I choked. Billowing dust was making it hard to breath.

Long Night with an Eight-armed Goddess

"Monsoons – they're late this year." He pulled a wax customs seal out of his pocket. "If they had been on time, you would never have gotten through central India."

Then, as he clamped the seal on the container door, the sky opened up and the monsoons were upon us.

Colin Bryant (left), Graham McGaw (right) and me with our Vauxhall Frontera in the Lut Desert, Iran, one of the driest places in the world.

41. Touch-and-Go Landing

The turbulence ended. I was looking out the window as the descending Boeing 747 finally broke through the overcast cloud layer. It was 2:45 in the morning.

"We must be at about 5,000 feet," I thought. "This could be just about anywhere."

From that height, all I could see were clusters of dull, flickering yellow lights looking more like sprawling army camps than the outskirts of a major world trading center. My partner, Ken Langley, was pulling out of a cramped, troubled sleep.

"Where are we?" he mumbled.

Outside the terminal, we turned down offers to purchase snake skin purses in favor of a beat-off taxicab.

"Started our descent into Bombay about 15 minutes ago. Have a look, that's India down there!" I said. "It looks innocent. But everything is different - the language, customs, religion, food. It's all down there, waiting to torture our bowels."

Ken didn't think much of that. His stomach was still unsettled from a night of debauchery in Kalgoorlie, Australia. My stomach was fine, but I was apprehensive. It was September 28, 1980 and Ken and I were into the 22nd day of an attempt to shave 37 days off the existing 104-day record for around-the-world driving. So far our trip from Toronto's CN Tower to Los Angeles and then across Australia had come off according to plan.

Red Cloud, our blue and white Halifax-built 1980 Volvo DL station wagon had run flawlessly. We were delighting our sponsors with plenty of good press and, with the exception of the finish-Australia-celebratory-mustiness Ken was feeling, our health was holding up. But now the Indian sub-continent was waiting.

The cargo people who had squeezed Red Cloud into the 747 in Australia warned us to keep an eye on the car until it was off-loaded. Since the Volvo had to be steered into and out of the aircraft's cargo hold, its doors had to be left unlocked. Apparently the Bombay Airport had a reputation for swallowing up cargo, so when we landed, the tools, cameras, spare parts, and other gear would be open prey for fast hands.

The aircraft was getting lower now, perhaps down to 1,000 feet. Thoughts of life below flashed through my mind as the big jet turned onto final approach. The yellow lights were closer but still flickering and dim. Then it hit - the stifling late-summer heat of the sub-continent started to seep in through the cabin pressurization system. It was

Throngs slept on the streets, sidewalks and in culverts. Trucks and buses were everywhere.

getting sticky inside when the aircraft touched down. Ken caressed his air-sickness bag.

When the flight attendant opened the airplane doors, a wave of hot, humid air consumed us and the other four disembarking passengers, then swept through the cabin over the 300 London-bound passengers who seemed relieved to be staying aboard. Ken and I descended to the tarmac where an airport official called us aside, introduced himself as the cargo manager, and ushered us into an immaculate 1959 Morris sedan. A stunning lady in a turquoise sari maneuvered the car to the other side of the aircraft where a dozen workers waited to off-load Red Cloud.

"We have only handled an automobile once before. Would you like to watch?" The cargo manager seemed genuinely excited by the task at hand.

An hour later, the disorganized crew had the car on the tarmac. The pilots, already late, gave a round of applause from an open cockpit window.

We were informed that the car wouldn't be released until Customs opened on Monday, 28 hours later. Nothing could be done so I scratched my head, locked the Volvo and we headed for the terminal building. Morning was a faint purple glow in the eastern sky. We were soaked with sweat.

Life in India was completely different than anything we had previously encountered on our around-the-world trip.

Outside the terminal, we turned down offers to purchase snake skin purses and whatever item strange hissing noises referred to in favor of a beat-off taxicab. On the way downtown to the Taj Mahal Intercontinental Hotel, we passed endless lines of people waiting for water and kerosene.

Throngs slept on the streets, sidewalks and in culverts. Trucks and buses were everywhere, lumbering around in the dingy dawn. The heat was making me itchy all over.

After not enough sleep, we awoke to significant surprises. The front page of the Bombay newspaper announced that war had broken out between Iran and Iraq. Ken's unsettled stomach had erupted into a full blown case of the dreaded dysentery. I discovered my torso had become home base to a colony of Australian body lice that most likely had climbed aboard during our debauched night in the Australian Outback.

Since remedies for both our ailments were conveniently stored in Red Cloud, I had good incentive to scratch off to Customs in hopes of an early release.

It took four days to get the car cleared. By then, our plan to transit Afghanistan and Iran had been scrapped. We would have to arrange for an airlift over the war and make up the lost distance by driving into the Scandinavian Arctic. Ken's dysentery was getting out of hand and, even with a fresh crew cut, the lice shampoo was a welcome sight.

The next morning at 3:15 a.m., we climbed into Red Cloud and departed the swanky Taj Mahal Intercontinental.

An hour and a half later, from a crest on the highway north of the city, I looked back and saw them again. But, with an unknown road ahead, those dull, flickering lights looked more like home than when I had first seen them a few days earlier.

Ken and I win the favour of striking government workers in central India.

42. *The Winds of Chance*

He had a diamond stud in his ear. I tried to remember which ear meant what, but it didn't really matter.

"What's the quickest way to get to the BBC studios?" I asked frantically. Sweat dripped from my brow.

He eyed the rumbling truck I had jumped out of as he tried to explain the zigzag route across Glasgow.

"Wha' doon't ye jes' folla me?" he wanted to know.

"I have no British money, I'm late and running out of fuel as we speak." I was starting to get into a real panic.

I had a bad case of navi-nightmare - an affliction brought on by temporary disorientation. It was usually associated with too much seat-of-the-pants navigation over unfamiliar roads. I was lost and I knew it.

I had forced over, and was presently interrogating, a confused-looking taxi driver. He apparently couldn't understand how a foreigner, driving a late model Canadian-registered pick-up truck, plastered with Spanish writing and maps of South America, wouldn't have a little local currency on hand to pay for guidance through the streets of downtown Glasgow.

"Yer on yer own, mate," he croaked, looking at me as if I could be dangerous. The diamond stud caught the faint February sunlight as he manoeuvered back into the traffic.

I had missed a turn when I leaned over and checked the auxiliary fuel level from the gauge mounted in the glove compartment. I couldn't believe my eyes when I realized I had already burned more than half of my fuel. I cross-referenced the logbook entries with the odometer reading, and realized I had only driven 934 miles. This meant I had less than half of the fuel left to cover the final 1,166 of the 2,000 miles that I was trying to drive ....without refuelling!

I couldn't believe my eyes when I realized I had already burned more than half of my fuel.

The plan was to drive from London to Land's End on England's pristine southern coast, up to John O'Groats on the windblown northern tip of Scotland, and back to London - without stopping for fuel. I had read a fuel economy tip claiming most motor vehicles burn about 23% less fuel at 60 miles an hour than at 75, and it made me think about the role that speed had played in the three long-distance driving records I broke in the 1980s.

I drove around the world, and from the bottom to the top of both hemispheres, faster than anyone had before. The only speeding ticket was somewhat of a donation to a bored Panamanian traffic enforcer en route to the Costa Rican frontier.

The success of these adventures was more the result of good planning, the right vehicles and a positive attitude, than of high speed. It seemed these were the basic ingredients of good fuel economy, so I decided to develop a challenge to demonstrate this. It would also force me to look more into fuel economy, a payback for the fuel I'd squandered over the years.

I already had a vehicle capable of such a job. It was the 1988 GMC Sierra pick-up truck that Tim Cahill and I drove from Tierra del Fuego, at the bottom of South America to Prudhoe Bay, Alaska in just under 24 days. The Sierra was already set up with an auxiliary fuel tank so we could hightail it through South American bandito country with minimal fuel stops.

Considering its overall fuel capacity of about 90 gallons, I figured the

183

8,000-pound rig would be able to complete the 2,000-mile loop of Great Britain without refuelling. I realized the 4-wheel-drive system and extended cab on the one-ton pick-up would cost me some fuel economy. The weight of the camper shell, extra spare tires, sleeping bunk and assorted paraphenalia would be a liability as well. But even with these handicaps, I figured the stock 6.2-litre diesel engine and its four-speed manual transmission would give me the 22.2 miles per imperial gallon I needed.

In London, a few days before the altercation with the Glaswegian cabbie, I made arrangements for a scrutineer from the Royal Automobile Club to seal the fuel system. After filling the tanks, he applied a special paint to certain joints, valves, hoses, pump mounts and fuel filtre brackets. After drying, the paint would crack if the fuel system was tampered with in an attempt to sneak more diesel into the system. He also combined wires and strange-looking metal clips to secure the fuel caps.

I planned a direct escape route from London on a Saturday morning that turned out to be a beautiful, clear day with the added luxury of a slight tail wind; no puddles or slushy roads to increase the rolling resistance. I could feel the weight of the extra fuel in the ride, throttle response, and braking effort. However, the big V8 diesel sipped at all that fuel like a seasoned miser, and I felt like I could get to Pakistan without stopping for fuel.

That night at the First and Last Inn in Land's End, I celebrated over a few pints, convinced that getting up to John O'Groats and back to London without refuelling, a mere 1,700 miles further, would be a piece of cake.

By noon the following day, the dash-mounted compass was pinned on North. I relaxed watching frisky spring lambs frolic about fluorescent green meadows while apple blossoms swayed in the delicate breezes, and rows of cackling black rooks schemed on the power lines.

I was contemplating British road signs when I first noticed the truck veering a bit to the right. Over the next couple of hours, while laughing about 'Get In' lanes, 'Dead Slow' areas and 'Way Out' zones, I noticed the flags in front of roadside service centres. Instead of fluttering in a gentle breeze, they were starting to look more like sheets of painted plywood, bolted to flagpoles as the wind from the north picked up.

Dark clouds filled the sky.

The wind was right on my nose. Sheets of blowing rain pelted the windscreen. With Birmingham just ahead, and Waylon Jennings on the tape deck wailing something about his heroes having always been cowboys, an incredible paranoia was unfolding in my mind.

"Isn't driving 60 miles-an-hour into a 50-mile-an-hour head wind really like driving 110? How much momentum are these raindrops robbing me of? What about all these puddles on the road? And what about the impetus lost when a mosquito or a fly, or a bumble bee splatters against the front bumper?" I wondered how all of this related to fuel consumption.

Vague recollections of college physics, fatigue and fuel-flow fascination were wrestling my brain cells as I pulled into Preston and stopped for the night.

In the morning, calm winds prevailed but by noon the plywood signs were back up the flagpoles as another gale raged from the north. I hated those flags. Not for what they symbolized, but because they were visible proof of the wind robbing me of the fuel - mocking my attempt to conquer the 2,000 miles without breaking the seals. I was starting to loathe those seals on the fuel tanks, too, as I headed for the BBC, took a wrong 'round-a-bout on the outskirts of Glasgow and found myself face-to-face with the disgruntled cabbie.

* * * * *

I was only a couple of minutes late taking my seat in the dimly lit radio studio.

"So you have had quite a history on the road setting all of these driving records," the cheerful host directed his questions enthusiastically. "And now you are over here doing what?"

I tried to sound keen as I explained my theories on fuel economy.

"And what about this pick-up lorry, or truck I guess you call it, that you are making the attempt in?" I was starting to squirm.

"Extended cab, 6.2L V-8 diesel, 4-wheel drive, modified fuel system," I gave him the stock answers.

"Well, tell us Mr. Sowerby, exactly how much fuel do you think you'll have left when you get back to London?" In my skeptical state, his sincerity sickened me. My stomach churned. I couldn't take any more.

"I pushed it too hard into the head winds and got lost a couple of times. I made a mistake with the calculations. I'm not halfway and have burned

Sightseeing was limited to attractions along the most direct route from Land's End to John O'Groats.

I headed north in the direction of Inverness through rolling hills, past abandoned castles, and over rambling streams.

over half my fuel." The rambling confession to all of Scotland helped me relax a little. "There's no way I'll make it."

I slumped in my seat as he urged me not to give up. He wished me all the best as he switched on Willie Nelson's *On the Road Again*.

"Forget the Loch Ness route," he advised. "Go northeast via Stirling and Perth. It's a few miles shorter and a lot flatter."

The rush hour traffic was building as Glasgow faded in the rear view mirrors.

I held the engine speed at 1,950 RPMs, peak torque for optimum fuel economy. The speedometer was steady at 51 miles per hour rolling along with the commuters. Snow and calm winds were predicted for the next day in the Highlands ahead.

That evening I checked into a small hotel right beside the road. The furnace was broken, but I didn't want to waste fuel looking around for another place to stay. It was a cold night in there, racking my brain over economical driving techniques.

I drifted into an uneasy sleep, aware that I had never been under such pressure to consider fuel economy. Usually it was only a matter of cash on hand, deciding which credit card to go for, or even finding a service station, that stood between an empty tank and more fuel. But having committed to this with other people's time and money on the line was good incentive to figure out how to manage the most out of every gallon. I simply couldn't run out!

At breakfast the next morning, my mind was racing again. "I need restaurants right beside the road," I thought. "No routing mistakes. Keep the speed down, but don't impede traffic flow."

"Er, excuse me, mate, but aren't you the chap trying to get 'round Great Britain without refuelling?" His eyes twinkled as he polished off his eggs and blood pudding at the next table. His white hair was slicked back. "Heard you on the BBC yesterday."

It turned out his name was Duke Windsor, and he knew the roads of Scotland like the back of his hand. He drew short cuts on my map and pointed out the level routes. He showed me his two-year-old Vauxhall pick-up with over 200,000 miles on it. He was in the courier business and loved the road.

"Don't worry lad, you'll make 'er!" he said. The Duke was a breath of encouragement all right.

I headed north in the direction of Inverness through rolling hills, past abandoned castles, and over rambling streams.

"Avoid aggressive starts. Remember every time I hit the brakes, I'm throwing fuel away. Keep calm," I mumbled under my breath. I knew all that, but was still tempted to shove the throttle to the floor and forget my fuel-miserly ways.

I stopped for lunch at a small roadside café overlooking the shimmering Dornoch Firth.

"Hey, you're that Canadian running out of petrol!" the waitress exclaimed, when I paid the bill. She was sure I'd make it. So was her boss when I met him in the parking lot, ogling the truck.

Before long, the only instruments of importance became the two fuel gauges.

"You'll make 'er," he said with a smile as he carefully centred the postmark in the trip log. It seemed everyone had heard my flaky interview on the BBC.

And so were the dozen construction workers widening the road on a series of hair-pin turns just south of John O'Groats. Twenty-four thumbs shot up as I passed, along with rousing cheers. I caressed the throttle, eyeing smoke drifting straight up from a distant farmhouse.

"No wind is better than a head wind," I thought.

There's not much at John O'Groats - a hotel out on a barren windswept point with a couple of quaint shops nearby. A mile inland is the tiny village with a few rustic homes scattered about. There's a post office whose charming postmaster stamped the logbook after I wrote a few postcards to friends back home.

"You'll make 'er," he said with a smile as he carefully centred the postmark in the trip log. It seemed everyone had heard my flaky interview on the BBC.

I sat in the truck in front of the post office with the engine shut off. The cab cooled quickly while I did a few calculations, extrapolations and estimations concluding that, even if the wind stayed dead calm, I would run out of fuel about 150 miles short of London - 650 miles to the south. Since the hotel at O'Groats was only open on weekends, I headed for Thurso, a small town 20 miles west along Scotland's rugged northern coast.

By the time I hit Thurso, I was convinced I really wouldn't 'make 'er.' With both gauges registering three-quarters empty, it appeared I was beat. The unforgiving eyes of failure stared me in the face.

I checked into a hotel in the quaint downtown where tidy rows of stone houses lined the streets. After freshening up, I decided to contact Weathercall, the British weather advisory service that had helped with some of the expenses of this trip. I couldn't believe my luck. A 40-knot wind from the northwest was forecast, with gusts of up to 70!

"I'm not moving until that wind gets here," I heard myself gloat.

The next morning I found a note tucked under the windshield wiper. *Hope you make it.* It was signed Cynthia, whoever she was.

The flag in front of the hotel was hanging like wet laundry when I left Thurso and headed south for Inverness. Fluffy snowflakes settled on large, hairy cows that stood motionless in nearby pastures. I featherfooted the throttle through the Highlands. The winds stayed calm, and so did I.

Just after noon while crossing the bridge into Inverness, I noticed a promising chop on Moray Firth. Further south the wind picked up even more, and I felt like I was floating on the welcome tail wind. Direction signs drifted past my periphery... Perth 20 miles, Stirling next right, Glasgow next left, keep left for Dumfries.

My stomach was growling, but I didn't stop at any of the roadside restaurants dare I waste the wind which marked its presence through starched flags pointing stiffly southwards.

My foot was barely touching the throttle. The speedometer was pegged at 58 miles per hour as the dual carriageway carried me past towns unseen - Carlisle, Preston, Birmingham. The Midlands were behind me, and the steady winds still leaned against the tailgate.

A road sign indicated that London was only 140 miles ahead. The auxiliary tank was empty and the gauge for the main tank indicated just more than an eighth left - about five gallons, I figured. The needle soon disappeared into the dashboard, yet that diesel engine still purred a fuel-stingy tune as I wound through the outskirts of London.

"Avoid aggressive starts. Remember every time I hit the brakes, I'm throwing fuel away. Keep calm," I mumbled under my breath.

Approaching Marble Arch, I couldn't resist pushing the throttle to the floor a couple of times.

"That one's for my stiff knee, this is for freezing in that hotel, and this is because I did it!" I was laughing, out of control.

Representatives of the Royal Automobile Club were on hand to verify that the seals were still intact. Then they followed me around the corner to a petrol station and watched while an immaculate Shell attendant topped up both tanks with a total of 86.86 Imperial gallons of diesel fuel. I had driven 1,901.8 miles over the five-day econo-cruise and had averaged 21.89 miles per gallon. There were less than 2 gallons of fuel left when I got back to London.

Looking back, the adventure had been an exercise in self-imposed stress. But with all the planning, the dedication to economical driving techniques, the scheming and the worrying, in the end I was saved by what had been my biggest enemy - The Wind.

43. *Mission to Moscow*

The burly policeman swaggered past me pushing aside the passports I waved in front of him, casually opened the driver's door and slid in behind the wheel. He seemed oblivious to the fact that someone was sitting in the passenger's seat. Then, leaning back, he grabbed the gearshift with one hand and wrapped his other calloused mitt around the steering wheel. Worn boots danced across the throttle, brake and clutch pedals as he slammed the shifter back and forth.

"It's a good thing I shut the engine off before getting out," I muttered to myself, slipping the keys into my jacket pocket.

Thick, windburned lips quivered under the intruder's scruffy black moustache as he imitated the sound of a racing car. Stubby fingers molested every switch, knob and button within reach. A fine spray of saliva appeared on the dashboard.

His partner stood beside me on the deserted road while my navigator,

Beverly Barrett, stared straight ahead from the passenger's seat. I wasn't sure if she was terrified, or if she feared the spectacle taking place behind the wheel was about to throw her into hysterics.

"*Spacibo,*" I said to our dubious guest. It was the only Russian word I knew and I pronounced it slowly, methodically.

"Whiskey," he replied, collecting his composure and climbing out of the truck.

I had a feeling things might get complicated following the two officers back to their cruiser - a faded red Lada with an awkward lean. A gleaming new radar gun, with '92' flashing on its digital display, was laying on the front seat. Just ahead of the unlikely patrol car stood a speed sign with '60' in the centre of it. The number was faded and small, about the size of a grapefruit.

"Please don't look in there," I thought, eyeing the combination lock on the tailgate of our grimy Canadian-registered pick-up truck. I could faintly see the outline of stacked boxes through the tinted windows of the camper shell.

A dialogue of Russian and English ensued. I was sure they understood as little of the exchange as I did.

Then, through a series of hand movements, facial expressions and body language, I convinced them that we didn't have any whiskey. My defense was entirely in English except for the string of *spacibos* I uttered backtracking, very slowly, to the truck.

"What did they say?" Beverly asked, as I pulled onto the road behind a smoke-belching transport truck. A Ukraine registration plate dangled from its tailgate by a single strand of bailing wire.

"I have no idea," I breathed in relief, shifting our overloaded rig into high gear. "But that *thank you* word you found in the guide book sure loosened things up."

****

Our personal travel documents were a bit shaky too.

We were on our way from London, England to Moscow by road in a four-wheel-drive GMC truck. It was the same diesel-powered pick-up I had driven from Tierra del Fuego, at the bottom of South America, to Alaska's Arctic coast in the record time of 23 days a few years earlier. The present trip was the result of a string of opportunities which began after shipping the truck from Canada to England to use in the British launch of a book Tim Cahill, my partner on the Pan-American trip, had written about that adventure.

In order to secure funding to ship the truck from my home in Halifax, Nova Scotia to England, I agreed to conduct a fuel economy test with it in Scandinavia. Since the test would start in Helsinki, Finland, I proposed to Beverly that we take a detour through Moscow where we could research a driving expedition across Russia and the new Republics I was considering. We felt somewhat guilty about driving an empty truck to a place in need of so many things, so we decided to look for something in England to take to help out the people of Russia. Ideally, it would be something for children.

In England we heard of an organization called 'Book Aid' that had collected more than a million English books to donate to libraries and learning institutions in Russia. The Russian airline, Aeroflot, had transported some of the books, but about a million of them were stranded in a warehouse at King's Cross in London. Some were children's books, so Beverly and I offered to take as many as we could to Moscow in the back of my truck.

We picked up 4,000 children's books from the Book Aid warehouse at King's Cross in London, England.

We managed to cram about 4,000 books into the truck, a lot more than we had anticipated. The down side was a complete lack of documentation regarding our payload. We would have to wing it, without customs or transit papers, through countless border posts and check points, not to mention legions of over-zealous radar-toting police.

Our personal travel documents were a bit shaky too. They consisted of passports along with Russian travel visas, which we arranged through a visa shop in London's Charring Cross subway station. Stapled to the visas was a faxed invitation to Russia from an organization in Moscow capitalizing on a loophole in immigration laws. We paid a fee equivalent to a few hundred dollars for the documents, which stipulated we enter the former Soviet Union at a remote border post in the southern Ukraine. That meant a roundabout route via Holland, Germany, Austria and Czechoslovakia before the long haul up to Moscow. Aside from the visas describing us as business consultants, we were armed with a single name in Moscow to whom we would turn the books over … Mrs. Geneva, Director of the Library of Foreign Literature.

The weight of the books, along with 96 gallons of extra diesel fuel we were carrying, left the truck sitting suspiciously low in the back. I figured it was just enough to tempt curious, or bored roadside officials to take a

We passed row upon row of identical high-rise apartment blocks that, from a distance, looked like giant doll houses rotting in a neglected yard.

cursory look inside our camper. As it turned out the first morning after leaving London, I was right.

****

"What's in those boxes?"

A cold grey drizzle was blowing on my face. A leather-clad Dutch customs officer had just watched me fumble with the combination lock on the tailgate and was curious about the cargo. He wasn't impressed with our lack of paperwork but bought the story about books for children in Moscow.

"I'll let you go this time," he warned. "The Germans won't be so easy though."

But the Germans didn't examine our payload. Nor did the Austrians, or the Czechoslovakians, who were more interested in issuing us $72 visas we didn't really need.

We reached the Ukrainian border without unlocking the tailgate once.

We paid a fee equivalent to a few hundred dollars for the documents, which stipulated we enter the former Soviet Union at a remote border post in the southern Ukraine.

****

The last piece of graffiti we spotted approaching the Ukrainian border proclaimed 'James Brown is free'. It was scrawled across the front of a sun-bleached cottage. A few hundred metres down the pot-holed road, a heavy blonde lady in a bulky uniform welcomed us to the Ukraine. Her icy blue eyes seemed to stare right through me. The area was completely void of signs except for a huge CCCP on the roof of a pallid two-storey cement building behind our reception committee.

"SUPER!" she exclaimed, breaking into a smile as she checked out the paint job on our displaced North American truck. Ten minutes later we were cleared into the country and went inside the CCCP building to exchange money. No one had looked in the back of the truck.

Once inside Beverly passed the lady behind the currency counter three American one-hundred dollar bills. The custodian of rubles examined the notes with a vague look on her face. She straightened out her short red crushed-velvet dress, which probably fit her

Russian school children were eager to practise English at every opportunity.

better years before, and handed the bills back shouting something to us in Russian.

"It's too much money," whispered an Italian businessman waiting in line behind us.

"But we'll be here for a couple of weeks," I told him. We're driving to Moscow and then up to Finland.

"Your truck will probably be stolen, vandalized for sure." His sincerity seemed genuine. It was a warning we had heard before.

We settled on changing $200 for 17,000 rubles, a three-inch stack of crisp new 50s. We felt like a couple of mafia dons walking out to the truck, which now lacked one basic Western motoring accessory - insurance. No one in Europe was keen to provide coverage for a Canadian-registered truck on an aid trip to Russia so we would try to buy insurance in Uzhgorod, a few kilometres down the road.

We slid into a dingy monochromatic world. Colour simply disappeared. We didn't talk much during the short drive to the sprawling city at the foot of the Carpathian Mountains. The road had an oily, slippery feel. The pollution made our eyes sting. We passed row upon row of identical high-rise apartment blocks that, from a distance, looked like giant doll houses rotting in a neglected yard. Limp, faded laundry hung from the balconies hopelessly waiting for the sun to cut through the thick blanket of haze that dulled the landscape.

We didn't have a road map for the 2,000-kilometre drive between Uzhgorod and Moscow. For a minute, I felt like turning around, giving the wad of funny money back to the flashy ruble lady, and taking the West European route to Helsinki. A thousand eyes pinned themselves on us while we cruised the broken streets of Uzhgorod looking for a hotel. I was imagining what an animal in a zoo felt like when Beverly noticed an Intourist hotel sign with an arrow pointing to a 12-storey monolith. A few bruised Ladas were parked haphazardly out front.

We maneuvered the truck into the guarded parking area behind Hotel Zakarpatie and ventured inside. A half-dozen attempts to communicate with as many hotel staff got us a room key. It came with an official visitor pass, which was diligently scrutinized by a uniformed elevator guard.

After dragging our bags to the room we found ourselves slightly dazed by a spectrum of pungent odors. It seemed the lobby, elevator, hallway and our room were safeguarded from visiting insects by a variety of insecticides. Adding to it was the overbearing perfume worn by ladies we passed en route.

"Let's freshen up and get something to eat," I suggested to Beverly, who was checking out the cavernous bathroom.

The water from the tap had an unusual green tint so we brushed our teeth with a bit of the gin I had stowed away in my suitcase. We took the elevator to the Hungarian Hall on the top floor where, apparently, we could dine to the music of a live band.

The Hall turned out to be the most brightly illuminated room I have ever been in. Music from a four-piece ensemble overpowered the roar of three hundred diners.

The maitre d' appeared. She muttered something I didn't understand, shrugged her shoulders and disappeared into the fray. We never saw her again. Soon, a portly expressionless fellow arrived and led us to a table beside the dance floor. He sat us across from a Russian couple we never managed to make eye contact with. The man stared silently at the table while his wife checked out the bottoms on the army of waiters scurrying about in what appeared to be a state of confusion.

We waited. The band played a few polkas. We waited some more. Finally a waiter zeroed in on our table. He was a lanky teenager, with thick rimmed glasses, dressed in a worn black tuxedo. I fumbled in English. He disappeared into the maze of tables.

Twenty minutes later, another waiter surfaced and gave us the hard sell for the grand meal; a five-course affair that would satisfy the most discriminating diner. His English was so perfect I suspected he was a former KGB agent. We passed on the grand one and settled for beers and two orders of fried chicken, a speciality of the house.

The beers were delivered promptly and tasted as if they were laced with ammonia. The band played *Tie A Yellow Ribbon* while a motley group of local he-men in fluorescent flared pants dragged their ladies through movements that would make Richard Simmons envious.

The dinners were eventually presented. They were grotesque. The single piece of chicken on my plate had been butchered in a way that forced one leg to hang off the bottom of the plate while an unplucked

It didn't take long for Beverly Barrett to get the hang of translating road signs from the Cyrillic alphabet.

wing stretched upward, well beyond the plate's upper rim. As I poked at it looking for a start point, the wing tip caressed my beer glass leaving a greasy little zigzag trail. At one point I tried to break the tangle of flesh apart with my hands and sticky pieces of fat and cartilage catapulted all over Beverly's legs.

"Road Kill Chicken," she hypothesized, washing down a bit of gristle with a mouthful of lukewarm ammonia beer.

In the morning the Intourist agent for the hotel presented our options. The city of Lvov was 250 kilometres to the northeast on the other side of the Carpathian Mountains. It did not have a hotel with guarded parking. This wasn't too appealing, especially after she informed us the only available insurance for the truck would cover damages we might inflict on Russian property and nothing else. If we were broadsided, the truck was stolen, vandalized or whatever, it would be our tough luck. Insurance was not something Soviet drivers knew anything about. It seemed an accident was simply an accident in their world.

With this in mind, the most logical option was to drive 220 kilometres past Lvov to Rovno where the Intourist hotel had a lock-up. Since driving at night was frowned upon by local authorities, and Rovno was a 10-hour drive, we hit the road without delay.

We got lost a couple of times on the way out of Uzhgorod. But Beverly soon learned to decipher the Cyrillic road signs with the help of a chart she found in a guide book, and we located the road to Lvov. Lingering banks of dense grey fog clung to the slopes of the Carpathian Mountains as we maneuvered along the winding, rutted road. Traffic was light, but the mud thick, and it took six hours to drive the 250 kilometres to Lvov. Since there were no direction signs in Lvov, we followed the streets with the most oil stains through the city of 750,000. We continued east on a much better concrete road.

It was evening when we arrived in Rovno. Beverly did a fantastic job homing us in on Hotel Mir, another cement Intourist hulk. The city had a weird feel about it – people bustling around in the darkness. There were no lit signs, no street lights. A few pale traffic signals flashed feebly while cars and trucks with blatting exhaust systems moved around in the dark like crickets prowling on a moonless night. I kept our park lights on and drew a host of flamboyant gestures from faceless silhouettes who probably considered us extravagant fools. In my imagination, I could hear air raid sirens wailing away.

****

With the truck secured in a fenced parking lot behind the Hotel Mir, we checked into our suite, a three-room affair decorated in arborite and polyester. A noisy fridge and a television that didn't work sat in the foyer. The restaurant downstairs was glitzy, in a worn 1950s style, with hundreds of huge plastic globes hanging from the ceiling. We feasted on fried potatoes, chunks of sturgeon, little beef cutlets covered with a tasteless black sauce and a mysterious salad while the band belted out crude renditions of Jimi Hendrix tunes.

In the morning, before departing Rovno for the Ukrainian capital of Kiev, I checked the combination lock on the tailgate. I brushed away some of the mud on the camper shell and could see the stacked boxes of books through the deep-tinted window. Three more days and our cargo would be safely at the library in Moscow.

During the long drive, the idea of a mechanical problem, or an accident was always on my mind.

We were getting attached to the books and the research we had planned to do for the future drive through Russia and the Republics began to take

Our day off in Kiev ended in the waiting room of a local hospital.

a back seat to our payload. We were in the middle of a strange, changing country financed with money I had borrowed with the now uninsured truck as collateral. We had a couple of questionable travel visas and a five-year old vehicle that had already been through its share of abuse in South America. We didn't have any spare parts and my tool box was conveniently located in the basement of my house back in Canada, 17,000 kilometres away. The truck was overloaded and my head was banging from our assault on a bottle of vodka the night before. We were operating on a thin line of faith in our ability to keep luck on our side, the battered Ladas out of our grill and the authorities away from our lack of paperwork.

"Take a right out of the parking lot and follow the buses," Beverly said in a hoarse voice.

It was a long drive to Kiev. We passed monuments of all kinds; factory workers with dedicated looks on their faces, jet fighters pointing toward the washed out, polluted sky. Birds of all shapes and sizes darted about stuffing twigs and pieces of trash between the branches of budding trees. The villages we passed were busy with Ukrainians sweeping and scrubbing away the dregs of the winter. Spring was on its way.

Kiev afforded us our first day off since we left England 11 days earlier. It seemed a lifetime ago. We went for a walk down a back street to escape the choking exhaust fumes of the Mother City of Russia's congested traffic. Beverly, suspiciously quiet all day, was commenting on the empty look on people's faces when she spotted a neon sign above a doorway. It was actually lit in the middle of the afternoon.

"Apollo," I said to Beverly. "I don't know what that means but let's find out."

Covered with a fresh coat of varnish, the door opened effortlessly, no squeaks. It didn't bind with the casing either. We slipped through the doorway into the West.

It seemed we had stumbled into happy hour at a trendy Chicago bar. IBM types sipped Tuborg beer out of frosty fluted glasses while a stunning blonde in a white silk suit toyed with a Remy Martin. She munched on fresh potato chips. Classical music played softly enough on a compact disc player that we could decipher fragments of quiet conversations in English, French and Italian. I ordered gin and tonics while Beverly pointed out that the bar stocked everything one could imagine, except vodka. A delicate white sign above the cash register read 'Hard Currency Only'.

"You're quiet today," I said to Beverly savoring the first taste of the gin and tonic. The rattle of the ice cubes sounded out of place in this land of elusive refrigeration.

She stared ahead, then down at the wedge of fresh lemon floating in her drink.

"I need some antibiotics. I think I have a bladder infection and it's getting worse by the hour."

Finding a cure for a bladder infection in the middle of the former Soviet Union seemed a formidable task. So we slipped back into the film noir world beyond the Apollo in search of a doctor.

****

The hospital was a white, two-storey structure with a thin blue stripe around it. Its reception area had five wickets serviced by ladies in uniforms that looked like something Florence Nightingale would have worn. We approached an elderly lady who appeared to be in charge. She was short with a mouth full of gold teeth and a smile that would put anyone at ease.

We realized the only term we had in common was the *thank you* word... *spacibo*. I tried to draw a picture of a bladder to no avail and we soon were following the nurse through a maze of corridors. She walked quickly, with a peculiar waddle.

She led us into a shabby examination room with a dull linoleum floor. A young boy sitting on a table moaned softly while a doctor pressed his hands into the child's abdomen. The physician could not understand us. Neither could the dentist installing a gold crown on a white-haired babushka, or the striking female doctor who made six telephone calls trying to help out.

The stairs to the top floor of the dimly lit hospital were dirty and worn. At the top dozens of people waited outside a single closed door. Men in uniform joked with young women holding babies. Old folks talked quietly with one another. Some stared up at a stained glass window depicting hockey players and a host of other triumphant athletes. Sunshine drifting through the work refracted into rainbows of coloured light that flooded

The Ukraine and Russia were both in dire need of a paint job.

the hallway. We followed our Mother Teresa to the front of the line and into the room beyond the closed door. It was obvious she carried a lot of weight in this hospital.

A stooped doctor checked out my drawing of the bladder. With his few words of English, we finally got the point of the infection across. He scribbled a prescription and passed it to Beverly. Then Mother Teresa led us out of the hospital and pointed to a building down the street which we assumed was a drug store.

"*Spacibo*," said Beverly, gripping the prescription.

Mother Teresa patted her gently on the arm, smiled affectionately and waddled back into the hospital. A few minutes later we handed .92 of a ruble to a pharmacist for a ten-day course of antibiotics.

"What a deal," Beverly remarked, walking back to the hotel. "We could have bought more than a thousand courses of those antibiotics with what we paid for our gin and tonics back at the Apollo."

In the morning we left Kiev for the first stage of the 700-kilometre drive to Moscow. We planned to overnight in a city called Oryol that apparently had a motel on the outskirts. But an hour south of Oryol, just after crossing the frontier between the Ukraine and Russia, we found ourselves in the company of the gear-jamming, radar-toting policemen who were so keen on Canadian whiskey.

"I guess we should have sent them to the Apollo bar back in Kiev," Beverly laughed, as they faded in the rear view mirrors.

The last few hundred kilometres to Moscow were monotonous and the closer we got, the more inquisitive the roadside authorities became. We were stopped every hour or so by officials looking for a vehicle document we had never heard of. One policeman showed us his own and was adamant we produce one before continuing to Moscow. But, once again, a series of *spacibos* got us on our way.

We pulled into Moscow about 2 o'clock on a Monday afternoon. The suburbs were crammed with commuters going who-knows-where in dilapidated buses. We maneuvered through the traffic to the centre of the Centre and checked into the Mezhdunarodnaya Hotel on the bank of the Moscow River.

I called the Library of Foreign Literature. Its director, Mrs. Geneva, was pleased to hear of our arrival. She asked us to drop by at noon the

next day, which would give her time to set up a reception with some media and representatives of the local libraries. She would also arrange for a few children to help unload all but a couple hundred of the books, which we wanted to give to an elementary school on the south side of Moscow.

Tuesday's reception at the library went well. There were plenty of handshaking dignitaries. Through an interpreter, we exchanged kind words about the end of the Cold War and the importance of education. They smothered us with gratitude for our efforts. Later, we drove across Moscow to the elementary school where a couple of hundred children, accompanied by a teacher who looked like the actor James Stewart, greeted us.

Beverly and I handed out the books and, just before we drove away, the teacher gave a signal to the children. They became very quiet and then, in unison, they smiled and shouted, "*SPACIBO!*".

44. A Little Gift Goes a Long Way

Toronto's CN Tower was less than 5 years old in 1980 when Ken Langley and I set off from its base in an attempt to drive around the world in 77 days or less. If successful, our trip would eclipse the existing Guinness Record for circumnavigation by car by more than a month.

Before leaving, the Tower's public relations people gave us ten miniature replicas of the Tower to hand out as gifts to special people we met along the way.

"Good to meet you Mr. Diplomat, Movie Star, King or President. Here's a statue of the CN Tower so you will remember the two yahoos from Nova Scotia who wanted you to grease the border so they could get a spot in the record books."

Later, while gloating over their graft, they could look in the Guinness Book of Records and see the CN Tower right there under world's tallest freestanding structure. Surely they would pass the gift on for their

We entered another huge city I had never heard of and negotiated our way through the creeping rickshaws, buses, bicycles and taxis looking for a place to spend the night

grandchildren's grandchildren to fight over.

The towers seemed a good idea until Ken and I had a chance to take a closer look at them near Moose Jaw, Saskatchewan on Day 3 of our big adventure.

They had to have been early prototypes of CN Tower models. The fake plastic marble bases supporting cheesy gold towers were tacky, to say the least. At the top was a plastic antenna that, when flicked with a thumb, would make a loud DOINNNG noise. Ken and I laughed like silly children over that noise. Imitating the sound after meeting anyone of any importance became an inside joke.

"Thank you for signing our log book, Mr. Mayor. Sorry we don't have the heart to lay one of the towers on you." DOINNNG. DOINNNG, and we were outta there.

By the time we finished North America and Australia DOINNGING had evolved into somewhat of a mantra in our daily routine. One of the foolish things that got us through our brutally hectic days. A little naughtiness that in reality wracked us with guilt as we sped around the world without giving a single one of the replicas away. I imagined us getting back to the CN Tower in Toronto where the media would be waiting. We would be heroes to the masses on hand. I could see us opening the tailgate and the ten replicas falling out in front of the Tower's PR people. We would of course be banned from Toronto and exiled back to the Maritimes!

To add to our confusion, most of the signs were in a script completely foreign to us.

Curious Indians took a keen interest in us as we passed through the towns and villages.

The evening of Day 27 of the adventure found us in central India. We had been driving since six o'clock in the morning and were into our usual Sub-Continental drill of three parts horn and one part driving. Accident avoidance was routine as packs of huge Tata transport trucks came at us filling the road like bad dreams.

We entered Jabalpur, another huge city I had never heard of, and negotiated our way through the creeping rickshaws, buses, bicycles and taxis looking for a place to spend the night. Most of the signs were written in local script so when we saw a dim neon light that read Jackson Hotel I yanked the wheel and drove through an archway into a tidy compound. A security guard saluted as we entered.

Inside, the quadrangle held a variety of businesses. There was the spartan hotel on one side. Another side was Jackson Hardware, another had bars on all the windows and the fourth side looked like a residence.

We asked about a room and were obliged with a spacious, clean suite with private bath and an air conditioner about the size of an Austin Mini that took the attendant 10 minutes of coaxing to fire up. Then he turned on an equally complex radio and proudly explained that the tune blasting very loudly was on the Indian Top Ten.

We unpacked and got cleaned up, rocking to the non-stop music. The cool room was a treat after the sweltering heat in the non air-conditioned Volvo. Soon a fresh-faced young man came to the door, introducing himself as one the Jacksons. He had been looking at our car and understood from the graphics on it that we were driving around the world. He would be honoured if we would meet his parents who were across the courtyard in the residence.

The interior of the house had a peculiar layout with no hallways. We went from one room to the next until, after six rooms, we ended up where Mr. and Mrs. Jackson were in bed propped up with ornate pillows looking very regal. They became quite excited to meet a couple of Canadians in the midst of their attempt to set a world driving record.

After a few minutes of pleasantries, I looked at Ken and discreetly flicked my thumb. Finally, a place to unload. I excused myself and negotiated back through the six rooms. I ran across the quadrangle to the Volvo and fished out one of the tower boxes.

I unpacked the tower to make sure it had not broken during the brutal shaking the Volvo had taken crossing the Australian Outback. The fake marble base shimmered under the interior light. I gave the antenna a couple of flicks with my thumb. DOINNNG, DOINNNG. It sounded the same as it did back in Moose Jaw.

I found my way back to the bedroom where Ken was waxing on about life in Cape Breton. I was going to give the tower a quick flick of the thumb as I walked into the room but thought Ken might lose it and we would look like a couple of jerks rather than big-time adventurers.

When I presented the tower to the Jacksons, Ken and I were surprised by their excitement. They seemed genuinely thrilled. The whole family started talking very loudly in their dialect. Mr. and Mrs. Jackson jumped out of bed and took the tower through a door on the far side of the bedroom.

We followed them through another three rooms into a stunning library. The walls were lined with hundreds of books. Lush carpets covered the floor. At the other end of the room, a stone fireplace with a wall-to-wall mantle held objects that were obviously treasured family heirlooms.

"This is unbelievable," I thought. "The tower really will be passed on from generation to generation signifying the time the rogue Canadian adventurers were in the Jackson household holding court with tales of life in Canada."

Then Mr. Jackson looked at Ken and I and smiled as he placed the gift on the mantle, beside another CN Tower… exactly like it.

Chapter 7 *Anyone Can Do That*

"What would you like?" asked the chatty bartender.
"We came for the toe," Lisa replied. The locals looked up from their drinks.

45. Serenade to a Drift-Jumper

I don't make a habit of visiting junkyards, but have a lingering fascination with them. A while back, I wanted an opportunity to get out of the office and away from the logistics and financial juggling associated with a motoring project we were planning. I also wanted to look at the other side of automotive assembly plants, showrooms and spec books. I needed to check out the end of the line.

I figured visiting seven auto junkyards in seven hours, including the Cyclomet - Eastern Canada's only auto-shredding device - would give me a chance to determine if my faithful winter drift-jumper, a then 15-year-old Oldsmobile Delta 88, was worth hanging onto for another winter's battle with the elements.

She was a rustic black dinosaur that had been hanging out with my fleet for years. The odometer had been around a couple of times, and in her early life she was obviously the recipient of many a fender-bender. A well-worn, likable old heap, her 403 cubic-inch V8 engine could easily rattle young men's egos at traffic lights when she shut down their high-

I needed to check out the end of the line.

The foreman's eyes sparkled as he told us how quietly the shredder did its number on the carcasses of family sedans.

revving GT coupes. She was the kind of beast other cars stayed away from at all costs, because she had nothing to lose. She sported half-worn, oversized Michelin tires, a taillight made of leftover stained glass from a local Baptist church, a perpetual sniff in the exhaust, a wimpy horn, and a clock that had read 8:23 for years. My kids called her Black Ugly because she was.

But she'd never let me down except for the time my ex-wife, who did her best to keep clear of the Olds, hit a pothole with it on the way to the mall. The confrontation resulted in the front door skin falling off and dragging along the street, dangling by the cables for the remote control side-view mirror. No big deal - I bolted the skin back on with carriage bolts that blended nicely with the overall ambience of Black Ugly.

So, in my quest to evaluate her right to another season of drift-jumping, I laid out a 300-kilometre route to a variety of potential resting grounds. First it was the premium yard of the Bastarache's. With a little coaxing, the quick-eyed foreman directed us to Olds Alley - a row of late-model, smashed-up beauties with a treasure trove of flawless quarter-panels, doors and bumpers. Too classy a joint for the Ugly one.

Then it was on to more informal yards that didn't seem as morbid because the 'inmates' weren't all late-model crack-ups. These places held the remains of cars that just wore out, gave up their craving to cruise to lounge around for years amid the alders, birch trees and wildflowers - where faded, worn-out relics could goof off and deteriorate without fear of the dreaded shredder. I liked those places, and thought Black Ugly wouldn't mind the setting for her final rusting place. By afternoon, we rolled into the Cyclomet yard, where row after row of flattened cars awaited the shredder and their journey to the smelter to be reincarnated as bridge girders, sardine cans or paper clips.

The Cyclomet's foreman looked the part: broken brown teeth, a bulging waistline, and greasy coveralls. He was a friendly, accommodating guy whose office was surrounded by a mountain of flattened yellow school buses. His eyes sparkled as he told us how quietly the shredder did its number on the carcasses of family sedans. Engine blocks were noisier. One flick of the switch and Black Ugly would be on her way to becoming three lumpy piles of ferrous metal, aluminum and 'fluff'. Forty seconds of muffled terror!

Among the devastation, somehow Black Ugly didn't look so bad anymore. After all, she had never burned or leaked oil and never got stuck where many others did. Feeling guilty, I took off for the fifth junkyard on my list, about 30 kilometres away. I was leaning towards keeping Black Ugly, so I pulled over beside a stream to collect my thoughts.

At first it was merely a malodorous presence. Then steam and finally a great green gush of antifreeze spewed forth as Black Ugly turned her radiator inside out. Had the Cyclomet been too much for her and she decided she'd rather die in the lazy sunshine beside the gurgling brook than in the jaws of the shredder? This was the first time she had ever failed me.

As I replenished the cooling system with soggy paper cups filled with the stream's murky runoff, I vowed to give Black Ugly one last chance. If she got me home, she'd live. If not - the shredder! Twenty minutes later, I pulled into my driveway as she blew again to the squeals and chuckles of the neighborhood children. A 403's cooling system in full-blown eruption was obviously a spectacular sight to those young kids.

I finished the junkyard tour in Red Cloud, the Volvo Ken Langley and I raced around the world back in 1980. Things weren't quite the same without Ugly though, so the next morning on my way back to brainstorming, budgets and Bulgarian visa applications, I dropped her at a radiator shop for a recore.

Then I laid her up for the summer to rest for yet another winter of drift jumping.

Among the devastation, somehow Black Ugly didn't look so bad anymore.

46. Smooth Operator and the Dent Police

The music was loud, especially considering it was only 5:45 in the morning. But the swagger of the bus driver was in perfect harmony with the beat. His biceps bulged as he effortlessly moved down the aisle, drifting suitcases into the side storage units with the precision of a laser-guided bomb. This was a man who obviously loved his job and the fact that the sun had just cracked the horizon was no detriment to his cheerfulness. The lyrics to the song fit this man to a tee.

"Smooth operator. Smooth operator… coast to coast L.A. to Chicago…" This mountain of a gent was the perfect catalyst to make you feel good to be alive.

Undeniably, this Hertz terminal transit bus at Chicago's massive O'Hare

Mr. Smooth Operator helps Gina Abram down from his magic bus.

airport was about the hippest people-mover I have ever been in. Blue-suit business types with perfect manicures, the Rastafarian up front and the couple in the back with the busy, toddling twin boys were all rockin' to the scene. And this Smooth Operator knew how to punch all the right buttons to make the short bus ride a memorable way to bid the Windy City good-day.

Actually my life had a lot more tension in it a few minutes earlier when I returned the flashy Volvo I had rented for the weekend. Sure it was dirty, even though it only had 600 miles on its odometer. But after all, isn't it a duty to make sure rentals get returned dirty? Dirty but blemish free has always been the motto which I have managed to live up to with the exception of a punched-out grill in a Lincoln Town Car after an altercation with an abandoned car in the fast lane of a foggy Interstate outside Detroit many years ago.

I'd rented the Volvo three days earlier in a torrential downpour to measure a drive route around Chicago for a program we were to produce later in the year. Since the sleek, fully-equipped Volvo only had 31 miles on the odometer, I figured there was no need to get soaking wet doing a walk-around looking for marks or dents. No, this baby was so new I felt like I was slipping into a pair of $500 Italian shoes for the first time.

Downtown I checked into Chicago's Park Hyatt Hotel. The concièrge pointed out a five million dollar painting in the lobby. It was alarmed to the teeth. There were plenty of staff sliding around, virtually unnoticed unless you needed them. I was taken to my room which was equipped with amenities that made me want to go into an immediate state of vegetation. Three telephones, surround-sound stereo, DVD player and two TVs including one on the bathroom ceiling where I could watch *Home Improvement* sprawled out in an impossibly huge bathtub.

Then the phone rang. It was Joe, the bellman. He was about to have the Volvo parked but wanted me to come down for a minute. Out front the car was sitting right where I had left it. Joe took me around to the passenger's side and showed me a small vertical dent on the rear door - up high, just below the window.

"Not me," I thought, visualizing someone cracking the door on the bones of the auto hauler that delivered the car to the rental car company. "But how will the folks at Hertz know that?"

*I **know** I didn't do it... really!*
I really didn't do it. Really.
Wasn't me.

Smooth Operator and the Dent Police

Thirty years of rentals and it all came down to this. Me against them.

Over the next three days I was haunted by that dent. It was the first thing I thought of departure day when the automated voice said *good morning* on my 4:00 a.m. wake-up call. As I cruised to the airport, that dent grew in my mind's eye.

Were aghast commuters pointing in the pre-dawn mist, "Look at that new Volvo with the trashed rear door!"?

Would the dent police be waiting for me with a mountain of paperwork? I could still see the lips of the agent who had rented me the car as she tried to convince me that, without the $24-insurance package, I was responsible for A N Y T H I N G that happened to the car.

I drove through the 'do not back up, severe tire damage' entrance gate. My palms were sweaty, my throat dry, and a knot was growing in the pit of my stomach. Thirty years of rentals and it all came down to this. Me against them.

As I parked, I told my associate Gina Abram to open the back door and stand in front of it. I felt cheap. A security car drifted by. Dent police for sure.

Then the cheerful check-in lady with the remote receipt device asked, "Full tank?"

"Yes," I croaked.

I felt like moving Gina from in front of the ding and confessing, "There it is. I'm coming clean."

She handed me the receipt and went on to the next customer. And as we walked to the bus I turned around for one last look. The morning sun caught the side of the Volvo but there was no dent. I moved my head from side to side. Yes, now I could see it. Barely.

We climbed aboard. The music was blasting. A sparkle of gold flashed as the driver mouthed a toothy "Goooood morning!"

"Smooth Operator, all right."

And I didn't do it, Mr. Hertz.

47. *Unplugged*

The flight from Los Angeles to New York's JFK airport was non-stop - five and a half hours of solitude in what had become a very hectic summer. Yes, up there streaking across the stratosphere was time to unwind, make notes on what had just unfolded and plan what's ahead. And one of the things that made it so peaceful was my refusal to use those sky telephones that are implanted into the backs of every second seat.

We landed right on time and I bolted for the car rental area to pick up my vehicle for a series of meetings in New York. Before exiting the parking lot, I did all the right stuff. I spread out the map and decided on a route that would get me to the hotel in the town of Rye near the Connecticut border. With the cellular phone plugged in and the mirrors adjusted, I found a rockin' radio station and then, for quick access, I laid out the notes from the airplane ride over on the empty passenger seat. There were a lot of them along with a list of people I needed to call. Their phone numbers were neatly printed in large numerals so they would be easy to read.

I noticed the guy in the next lane wagging a finger at me.

"Use me, use me now!"

I ended up doing two loops around the airport Arrivals level before finding my way out of the massive JFK complex and onto the Van Wyck Expressway. Then I called the hotel to get detailed directions. In the middle of the conversation, I noticed the guy in the next lane wagging a finger at me. It wasn't a rude gesture that someone you just cut off might flash, but a side-to-side motion as if I had done something naughty. I nodded, smiled and carried on.

Then I called Lisa to tell her I was only one time zone away. She filled me in on the status of life in Halifax while another motorist gave me the 'phone sign' - thumb in the ear, three middle fingers clinched and the pinky close to her lips. She gave me a bit of a nasty look, too. That's when I remembered reading something about New York's new law prohibiting talking on cellular phones while driving.

All of a sudden, I felt dirty. I cut the call and stared ahead. I was stunned. How could I exist for the next ten days without talking on the phone while piloting two tons of metal through some of the most congested roads on the continent? What about the call list I had so diligently prepared up there over Nebraska? And what about all those people who just *had* to hear from me? After all, I was on the ground and it was my right to let half the planet know.

OK. I put the phone down. It seemed to scream, "Use me, use me now!" Looking around in the congestion, I couldn't see one person on a cell phone. Lane upon lane of creeping traffic, prime cell phone territory, and nobody on a phone. What could all those commuters be doing in there?

Then it hit me. Relax, Garry. I changed the radio station from the doo-wop oldies to a classical one and thought about driving before cellphones, back when getting in your car was getting away from it all.

The road was a place where you were on your own. It was a haven where no one could get in touch with you except through one of those radio announcements looking for someone who needed to call home for an important message. Time was spent considering the big picture instead of dealing with all the small details phoneaholics like me have to be constantly worrying about.

I thought about that 'out of contact' all-night road trip between Ottawa and Halifax in 1977 when Ken Langley and I dreamed up the idea of driving a car around the world in record time. Not for everyone, but it sure changed my life. On that expedition, Motorola supplied us with the latest in mobile communications and although we only managed to complete 3 successful calls in 74 days, we still shaved more than a month off the record.

Then in 1997, during another around-the-world drive, the latest in mobile communications let us send and receive e-mail, fax and a zillion telephone calls. At times it was like a virtual trip around the world. Lots of information on the go, but in reality a boring trip compared to when Ken and I were out there out of touch.

I began to relax, creeping along with the New York evening commuters and over the next week, I got used to driving rather than running a mobile office. Once in a while, I would forget and find myself dialing up a number but would stop, pull off on a side street, and watch kids play while using the phone.

Once, pulled over into the parking lot of an abandoned amusement park, I was chatting to my travel agent about changing a flight. I got a beep and transferred to the incoming call. I was staring at the bumper-to-bumper mess out there on the Bronx Expressway when I heard my twin brother Larry's voice.

"What's up?" I asked. "And what's that racket in the background?"

"Just cruising up the Saint John River in the new motorboat." He was excited to be on holidays visiting our old friends Joe and Pat Tippett.

We chatted. He handed the cell phone to Joe and we laughed about old times. Then I hung up, fired up the rental car and headed back into the fray. I thought about New York's new cell phone law. I grinned, realizing that law had a long way to go before reaching the backwaters of New Brunswick.

"C'mon... just one call... it'll make you feel good... it's so convenient..."

48. Rocky-Go-'Round

For the past 25 years I've been involved in developing more than 75 driving events, some in rather improbable parts of the planet.

My colleagues and I have broken the around-the-world driving record under both the one and three-driver rules. We have put a car on top of the CN Tower, smuggled a truckload of children's books to Moscow schools and raced a truck around the perimeter of Iceland in the dead of winter. We've set records for the quickest time from the bottom to the top of Eurasia as well as the Americas.

For a guy who loves to travel and is fascinated with motor vehicles, I have managed to have my cake and eat it too. But, every now and then, I find myself wanting to do something that doesn't have to be reinvented every day. Do a routine driving job for a while, like those people who drive the subway trains, courier delivery trucks or the car rental company buses at busy airports. Get up in the morning, kiss the wife goodbye and go do something that involves moving a wheeled piece of machinery

I kept back so they wouldn't feel like Dad was stalking them to make sure they weren't out pruning the family wheels.

around the same place. No brain cramps. No maps. Nothing unfamiliar.

In the summer of 2001, I got an opportunity to do just that … sort of. Ford Motor Company wanted to give some of their customers, who'd been patiently waiting for their all-new 2002 Thunderbirds, a test drive in one of the 252 hp rockets. Lisa and I were asked to develop a 40-minute drive route around the suburbs of Detroit. We chose an area north of the city, through the upscale hamlets of Birmingham and Bloomfield Hills. Good back roads, a little freeway work and a section through a trendy shopping and dining area where the T-Birds would be the focal point of much 'rubbernecking'.

The plan? Every hour, five couples would arrive at the start point and, after a short orientation briefing, would set out on a 20-mile route that we had mapped out. They would use basic rally instructions, which called for them to match odometer readings with simple written instructions.

My daily routine? Wake up call at 4:45 a.m. Moan. Lie around like a beached flounder for 15 minutes, then a 30-minute jog down Big Beaver Road. Back to the hotel for a flash shower. Down to the breakfast room to choke back some of the free breakfast buffet before the 10-minute drive to the start point at the swank Bloomfield Hills Open Hunt Club which, these days, caters to the horsey set and has nothing to do with hunting. Once there, we would detail, stage and prep five of the brand-

At this point, I'd passed the Birmingham Cinema 38 times...

new 'Birds and wait for the first driver crews, mostly couples that approached the racy Thunderbirds as if reuniting with a long-lost love.

During the four days, I followed them around the course more times than I could count, logging almost the distance from New York to Chicago. The route meandered through posh neighbourhoods canopied with lush vegetation. On the first run, I noticed fresh roadkill on the side of the road, a deceased raccoon slowly baking in the sun as the smiling T-Birders cruised on by. Meanwhile routine-man me kept back so they wouldn't feel like Dad was stalking them to make sure they weren't out there pruning the family wheels.

At the end of each drive, we listened to raves about the car while I took stock of the next teams. Another briefing. Back in the chase vehicle. Check out the ripening Rocky Raccoon. Don't let them see me in the rear view mirror and hope the emergency cell phone didn't ring.

It did a few times, but never for anything serious. Some teams had ignored the basics of a written drive route - like 'trust the navigator' and 'don't follow the car in front'. On one occasion, instead of our prissy route, occupants in a convoy of three T-Birds got a first-hand look at the back end of one of GM's truck assembly plants. One lady, with her 88-year-old mother navigating, ended up in a Wal-Mart parking lot on the other side of Detroit.

… make that 39 times.

But, for the most part, all went according to plan while I checked out Rocky nine or ten times a day. I got so accustomed to the route that the idea of diverging from it was right up there with pulling headfirst into the oncoming traffic or throwing the transmission into reverse at road speed. I soon knew the shift points of the new Explorer I was driving, counted the 37 rumble strips at the third traffic light and became an expert at the 'Michigan Left'. I memorized every word on an old-time gospel CD I picked up in a five-dollar sale bin at K-Mart. *Swing Low, Sweet Chariot!*

On the last run, I had a feeling something would be different. The participants were still smiling and thrilled with the sleek Thunderbirds. The rumble strips were still rumbling. But when I passed Rocky Raccoon's place on the shoulder of Long Lake Road, there was nothing but a dark stain. The roadkill clean-up crew had been on the prowl.

I knew it was time to go.

Thunderbirds at the Bloomfield Hills Open Hunt Club awaiting another group of drivers.

49. Long Haul Down Rebuild Road

I've always wanted a 1965 Ford half ton pick-up truck. My dad bought one after starting a plate glass and storefront contracting business in the mid-1960s when I was 16 years old. Even though there was a new Mercury Parklane in the driveway, my vehicle of scrounge for those high school years was that gunmetal grey truck. It had a 352 cubic inch, 220-horsepower V-8 engine, a three in-the-tree column shifter and the all-new 'Twin I Beam' front suspension. An optional $35 body-length polished aluminum molding stretched along each side from the front of the hood to the tailgate.

I used it for dates, cruising the strip and hauling garbage to the dump from time to time. It was one of the only V-8 pick-ups in town, and after

its work week in the glass business, I'd detail it for Saturday night junkets.

In 1996, while planning a cross-continental trek for an auto manufacturer, I spotted a similar 1965 model at a radiator repair shop just off the main drag in Bandera, Texas. It was blue but had the same options as the one my father had, so I left a note on a business card, inquiring if the owner was interested in selling.

Three weeks later, a lady from Bandera called. The dog breeder, who had owned the truck for 30 years, had just bought a new V-10 Dodge extended cab and was willing to part with the old Ford for $1,500. I didn't even try to beat her down.

She recommended a local bodyman who, for reasonable compensation, would paint the faded, rust-free truck gun-metal grey. I wired her the money and made arrangements for the truck to be left at the body shop. A month later, I flew to Texas to find my purchase in a discouraging state of disassembly. After a week of coaxing, Mr. Bodyman, who seemed more adept at bingeing than bodywork, slapped the old beast back together. Then I headed off on the 5,000-kilometre drive home to Halifax.

An hour out of Bandera, the engine dropped a valve so I spent the next 4 days baking inside the 31-year-old sweatbox, half expecting the engine to self-destruct. Meanwhile, I felt like King Yokel pulling into service centres in the sputtering, half-primed eyesore, sweating like I had just run the New York Marathon. But even with the engine running on 7 cylinders and the 8-track tape deck seized, I was starting to love that truck.

When I got home I had the engine and most of the drive-line rebuilt. It definitely lacked social acceptability, but the old truck ran like Jack the Bear. I tracked down a place to purchase many original parts for the body and interior. Windshield-mounting rubbers, cat's whiskers for the door

These instruments of nostalgia bring me back to when I first learned to drive.

*When I picked it up a year later,
the only thing that had been
repaired was the tailgate.*

windows, tail-light lenses and a new rubber floor mat were ordered along with two large boxes of bits and pieces. Then I drove 1,800 kilometres to Toronto where a body shop that had done another job for me agreed to work on it in their *spare* time.

When I picked it up a year later, the only thing that had been repaired was the tailgate. The rest of the truck looked as rugged as it did when I had dropped it off. I had owned it for almost 2 years and, except for the tailgate, it still looked the same as when I pulled out of Bandera.

Back in Halifax I met Bryan Jones, a former musician, who augmented his income by meticulously restoring one or two vehicles a year. He agreed to finish the pick-up if I could leave it with him for six months.

"Where do you start?" I asked, eyeing the gnarly rig parked inside Bryan's humble back-yard shop.

"I take a door and I work on it until it's finished," he explained, rubbing the tailgate with a disapproving look. "When it's done I take another door, then a fender or the hood. I don't get wrapped up in dreams of completion. I enjoy each piece and do the very best I can until my progress eventually motivates me through the bits I don't like to do."

Over the next few months, while out setting a new around-the-world driving record, Bryan's advice helped keep up my morale. When I'd get into a funk feeling like the road from Tehran to New Delhi would never end, I'd think about Bryan back home re-doing the tailgate. One piece at a time. Make the most of getting to New Delhi before thinking about the next leg of the journey.

Bryan finished the job on time with the exception of the grill and front bumper that required a mysterious 'Wimbledon White' paint. So I moved the truck back into my garage where it sat for two years when I finally installed the last bits and got it on the road.

The following morning, I cleaned out the garage and decided to take a load to the dump. Lisa was keen to get in on the big event. It was the first real job for the truck and I felt a sense of accomplishment. The old Ford had turned out even better than expected and I finally had a pick-up truck. The purr of the dual exhaust, the view out the windshield and the feel of wrapping my arm around the steering column as I slid the transmission into second gear brought me back to my youth.

"You know, Lisa." Guilt reared its wimpy head. "This truck ended up being a lot more work than I ever imagined… bringing it home from Texas, the engine, all those new parts, repairing the 8-track cassette player, two trips to Toronto. Three body shops, for Pete's sake!"

I was having a hard time fessing up to myself, let alone my unsuspecting mate.

"When I add it all up, I probably could have bought a new truck," I offered sheepishly.

"Well, anyone can do that!" she fired back.

Bryan Jones' philosophical outlook on bodywork came in handy while driving around the world.

50. Bombay Peggy's and the Sourtoe Cocktail

Things didn't sound quite right at the Pelly Crossing filling station in the middle of the Yukon Territory. The gurgle of the fuel I was pumping down the filler neck had a frothy note, reminiscent of the sound of filling up one of the diesel pick-ups I've owned over the years.

I smelled the nozzle before I hung it up and, at precisely the instant my nose processed the 'Diesel-you-idiot' warning, my eyes focused on the word DIESEL on the front of the fuel pump.

To say I felt stupid was an understatement. The gasoline-powered Chevy Blazer I'd rented from National Car Rental in Whitehorse obviously would have to have its tank drained and the delay would cut the heart out

of the mere six hours of daylight that mid-December offered at this latitude. It might even disrupt overnight plans at Bombay Peggy's, a renovated former brothel in Dawson City, where Lisa had reserved the Lipstick Room.

"There's a silver lining though," I tried to be upbeat as I confessed the fueling blunder to Lisa. "It's Friday the 13th and this should be enough of a screw-up for clear sailing at Bombay Peggy's along with my quest to be ordained into Captain Dick's Sourtoe Cocktail Club."

Lisa realized how sheepish I felt. The affable lady at the service station told me lots of people had filled their gasoline cars with diesel fuel there. Her boyfriend, David, had the day off and could be on the scene in a few minutes. He had helped out some of the other 'fuel losers' here on the Klondike Highway between Whitehorse and Dawson City, just south of the Arctic Circle.

David arrived and after two hours of coaxing, we managed to siphon most of the fuel out of the tank. We refilled with gasoline and headed out into the afternoon twilight.

We arrived in Dawson City, a town of 1,900 people, that was once the largest city west of Winnipeg and north of San Francisco. Bombay Peggy's turned out to be a lovingly restored Inn that had been a bustling bordello. After 535 kilometres of icy roads, snow squalls and the diesel fuel fiasco, the friendly hosts and lush appointments of the Lipstick Room were a welcome change.

Owners Wendy Cairns and Kim Bouzaine breathed new life into an old brothel.

After an hour of rest, the Sourtoe Cocktail beckoned so we left the cozy hotel and moseyed across town to the Sourdough Saloon located in the Downtown Hotel. The streets were deserted. The lonely sound of our boots on the wooden sidewalk reminded me of a cattle rustler heading to the gallows in a 1950s western movie. What had I gotten myself into with this Sourtoe Cocktail?

The Sourdough Saloon wasn't much livelier than the wintry streets of Dawson City. Three locals sat at a table hunched over glasses of draught beer. Lisa and I approached the rustic bar a few stools down from the only other patrons, a grizzled couple whispering sweet nothings to each other.

"What would you like?" asked Donna Nickerson, the chatty bartender.

"We came for the toe," Lisa replied. The locals looked up from their drinks.

"The toe or the full foot?" Donna went on to explain that the full foot consisted of 5 toes rather than just one big toe.

"Just the toe."

I felt a lump in my throat and considered bolting back to the comfort of the Lipstick Room. Donna produced a small crock, undid two metal fasteners and pulled the top off, revealing a mound of coarse salt.

"Now I gotta dig for it," she said with a smirk.

There was no doubting what it was: a hefty-sized big toe, nail and all. My stomach heaved as Donna explained that the drink I chose should

I stared at it for a long time before making my move.

not have any ice in it. I wondered if the toe would sink or float. When she plopped it into a glass of water to rinse off the salt, I averted my eyes.

"After I put it into your cocktail, I have to see the toe rubbing against your lips as you drink." She seemed to enjoy the ritual.

My last thought before imbibing was to wonder if it was poisonous, but surely I would have heard about Sourtoe casualties on *Fox News* or seen bizarre headlines splattered across the front cover of a *National Enquirer* at a supermarket checkout somewhere.

I tipped the drink back and eventually felt the grotesque appendage rub against my top lip. The more I drank, the more toe pressure I felt.

"No one can take it from me now," I thought as Donna declared me 'Sourtoed'. I thought I heard a sole handclap. It was over. What taboos had I violated?

On the walk back to Bombay Peggy's, I examined the authentication certificate Donna had presented to me. I was Club Member #12,224. There's even a web site where non-believers could get more information. I smiled to myself thinking that kissing a cod in Newfoundland had nothing on this Yukon ritual.

My mind drifted to the cozy Lipstick Room just as Lisa assured me my toe-touching lips were not high on her list of priorities. I slipped my arm around her shoulder trying to warm things up.

"Your sleeve smells like diesel fuel!" She muttered.

I looked at my watch. Ten-fifteen. It was still Friday the 13th.

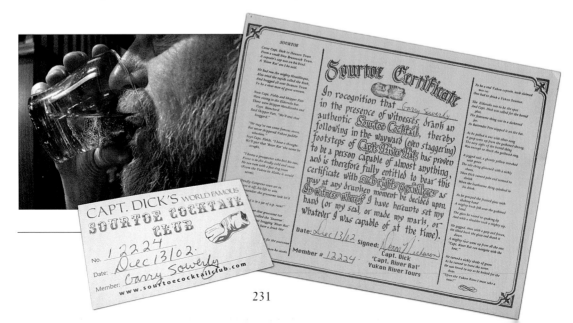

Story Timeline

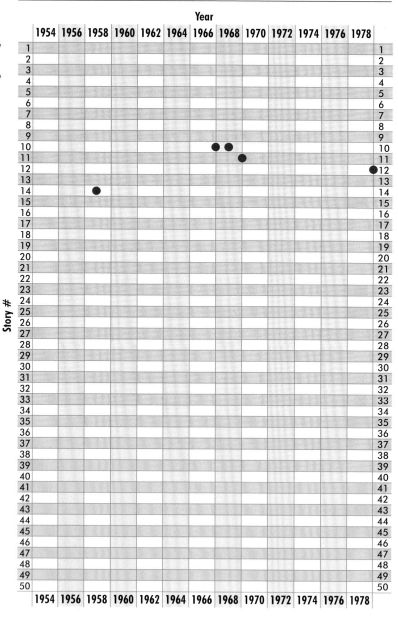

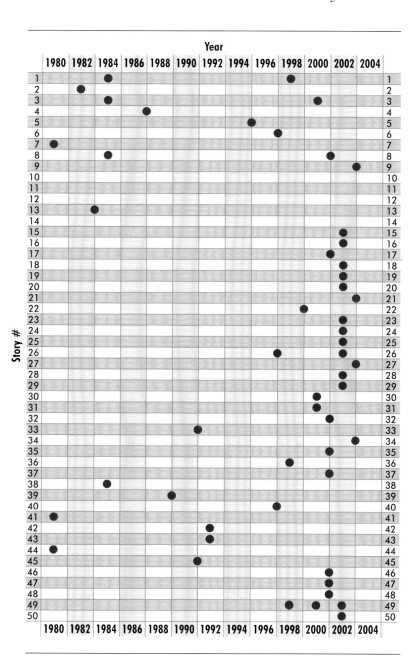

Story Timeline

233

Photo Credits

All photography and images by Garry Sowerby or
Odyssey International Limited except the following pages:

Richard Sala, illustrations 12, 14

Lucy Sowerby, illustrations 15, 16, 17

General Motors of Canada Limited, bottom photograph 37

Oldsmobile History Museum, photograph 50

Paul Fleet, top right photograph 75

Karen Ramsland, bottom photograph 83

Richard Russell, bottom photograph 111

Chad Heard, top photograph 113

Lars Gange, photography 114 - 117

Rik Paul, photography 121

Philip Baird, photograph 176

Hollywood Photography, Moscow, photography 202, 203